WHEN THE MIRACLE COMES SLOWLY

WHEN THE MIRACLE COMES SLOWLY

Beatriz Benestad

Sovereign World

Published by Sovereign World Ltd
PO Box 784
Ellel
Lancaster
LA1 9DA
United Kingdom

www.sovereignworld.com
Twitter: @sovereignworld
Facebook: www.facebook.com/sovereignworld

Published April 2016

Originally published in Norwegian under the title
Når underet kommer langsomt
by Lunde Forlag, Sinsenveien 25, 0572 Oslo, Norge

Translation by Marie Hansen

ISBN: 9781852407872

Cover design and typesetting by www.zaccmedia.com

Printed in the United Kingdom

BENEATH A BLUE GUAYACÁN

Everyone knows that guayacáns have yellow blossoms.
Only my guayacán is blue.
It has the colour of a tropical sky
arching above the blazing day.
It is deep blue as the oceans deep,
where seven different shades of blue
wash away all sounds from the surface.
It is blue as the lonely sorrow of dark night hours.
It is blue as the sparkling joy of being alive.

Contents

Author's foreword

How God can use a small person in an impossible situation

It is January 1st 2014 – the first day of a new year that stands before me with blank, empty pages and endless possibilities. I am in Colombia in South America. This is where I have lived for almost twelve years. As a medical missionary in a wheelchair I have had to adjust to a completely different life than that which "welfare" Norway can offer people in my situation.

To begin to write a book about how all this came to pass is like starting an archaeological excavation. First of all, there is a lot of dirt that needs to be dug up and removed. Then, as the discrete objects become visible, they must be dusted, cleaned and categorized. Fragments of objects that seem to have little value may hold the key for a deeper understanding. Other things are put aside – either because they lack meaning, or because they are too fragile or difficult to handle.

Little by little a story unfolds. A story about the past, about the people who played a part, and about the incomprehensible. For me this story is about small beginnings and great visions. It is an account of how God can use a small person in an impossible situation. The Bible tells us that nothing is impossible for God. I believe this! He carries me when I am incapable of taking another step. He comforts me when weeping surrounds me in endless nights without rest. And He takes delight in my joy. He is my Father. He is my friend. He is my all!

This book is dedicated to all those who struggle through heavy days – all those everyday heroes who are never praised, among them Irene, Hedwig and Berit who went to be with the Lord before time. This book is about the life that is lived when the miracle *doesn't* come drifting downwind on a hot summer's day. It is about a journey, hand in hand with the Lord of Life, when the journey and life itself is a miracle.

My gratitude goes to Peter and Fiona Horrobin, founders and leaders of Ellel Ministries International. Thank you for giving me confidence and for believing in all the projects that were initiated over the years! I also thank Dag Gundersen Storla, friend, colleague and author, for his unshakable faith in this book project, and for opening the necessary doors. Furthermore I am immensely grateful to Jostein H. Sandsmark in Lunde Forlag for taking on the job of transforming my manuscript into the book you are holding in your hands. Thank you for your great kindness, patience and lots of encouragement along the way! Special gratitude also goes to Rosalinde Joosten from the Netherlands, who found out how Norwegian letters are entered into a Colombian pc. I additionally want to thank each and everyone who has let me take part in their life experience, both the good and the painful. We have all experienced how the road unfolds as we travel.

In consideration of privacy and security in Colombia, I have chosen to give some of the individuals mentioned fictitious names. A few times names of places have also been changed.

Most of all my deepest gratitude goes to my Heavenly Father, the one who saw possibilities where no one believed in a path ahead. By His hand this book came into being. For this reason all honour goes to Him! I myself am only a writer who has jotted down thoughts of how God paved the way for me and my work, and how it all happened.

May you, who sit with this book in your hands, be richly blessed on your own path of life as you read about my days underneath a blue guayacán – and the road that brought me there.

Beatriz Benestad

1

Dreams

It is very early morning. The snow falls silently over naked black birch branches outside my window. The gloom has a soft grey clearing, signalling the approach of a new day. It is the dark season, at the end of December. A cold and chilly day is inclining against the window outside.

I open my eyes slowly. I can still feel the touch of the warm wind against my cheeks and the vibrating heat in the shadow beneath the tall, strange tree. I still hear the laughter of children in the distance. Rather slowly I am coming out of my sleep.

It is the second night in a row with dreams. Last night I dreamt that I was sitting next to an airplane window looking out upon a landscape of high mountains. Some of the mountains were covered in snow. Everything was coloured in a pink yellow hue that made me think of sunsets. In the dream I was eagerly talking to a smiling person who was standing right in front of me. I was pointing out the landscape as we flew above it, as if it was familiar to me. Together we gazed with expectation at the mountains.

Both dreams were in strong colours. Moreover, they gave me the sensation that they were related to real places and situations.

My daily life is anything but a dream. I am seventeen years old and find myself in my childhood home at Hadsel Island in Northern Norway. In real life I have never been outside the borders of Norway. The only planes I have travelled in are small seaplanes. I will graduate from high school in the coming summer. After that the plan is to have a series of surgical procedures done at *Revma*, the hospital of the Norwegian Sanitation Foundation for Rheumatism in Oslo. There I will receive "new" hips. I have juvenile arthritis, and now misalignments and pain will be relieved by the latest national achievements in orthopaedic surgery. After that I have plans to study medicine.

I am a born again Christian. In the Bible I have read about Joseph and his strange dreams that were all related to a distant future. Are my nightly dreams also visions about something that may happen at some time? Something that *will* happen? Something that is planned according to God's purpose?

Throughout the next twenty-seven years these dreams will be repeated many times. Every time I notice – and remember – more and more details from the dreams. For example that the children in the second dream are playing with two balls, a red and a green, and that the children have facial features which indicate that they have Down's syndrome. Behind them I see white houses. The tree I am standing beneath has thin branches spreading out in different directions and a canopy of small leaves. It reminds me of an umbrella without the fabric.

The dreams are always the same. Each time they are repeated, it is as if they draw closer. The first time, I see the landscapes as on a movie screen. Finally, I am not just a spectator but see the pictures through my own eyes. After a few years I no longer doubt that they concern me and my life – my own future. It is something important, that God has planned for me.

When I consider your heavens, the work of your fingers,

the moon and the stars, which you have ordained,

what is man that you are mindful of him,

and the son of man – that you visit him?

Psalm 8, 3–4

2

Early childhood memories

I can still remember the day the first pineapple arrived. Aunt Tutti, who was a flight attendant, brought this exotic treasure home. For many weeks it was ripening on the window sill, while we, the children, were beholding it with reverent respect. We had never seen anything so perfect before! The round, sweet-smelling, yellow globe with small spines and a little green tree on the top – it was a wonder!

When it was time to attack the pineapple, the experience was almost *too* exciting. The taste was amazing! Sweet, sharp and unknown. The long ripening had, however, damaged the fruit rather than improving it, so only a small part of it was edible. Still, it became a heavenly foretaste of the tropical tastes of the future. The ice cream that we froze in the pile of snow outside the kitchen window could not compare to our special pineapple.

I grew up in post war Norway. Even in the late 1950s there was still a lack of several things. When I was a child, it was common to have shortages of certain food items in Northern Norway.

Then there were our clothes. The homemade, thick and itchy wool sweaters were not very popular. It was however necessary to have thick clothing in the cold winter. "Luggene" were such necessary footwear. They were like thick long socks, with layers of wool felt sewn together as soles. In dry and cold winter weather they worked well as boots.

Winter was a wonderful time. My brother Rolf Kristian and I would play in the banks of snow. We made snow lanterns with small snowballs, and at night candles were lit in the lanterns. Then we would look out proudly on our creations. Other times we would lie on our backs in the snow and make "angels" by moving our arms and legs out to the side. My brother became very good at skiing. I was more careful, but found great enjoyment in the sledge, toboggan and my own little kick sled. One of my fondest memories from this time is of a kick sled ride with my dad, Håkon.

In Northern Norway the dark season lasts through many long winter months, and the northern lights can dance across the dark sky like translucent, multi-coloured curtains hung by a large hand. Dad and I would go coasting ahead on sharp runners in the dark winter evening, sometimes only lit by the stars and the reflection of the white snow, other times also with the northern lights across the sky. Dad would often stop to point out the star constellations for me – the Plough, Ursa Minor and Ursa Major, the Pleiades and Orion's Belt. He told me about the legends that were attached to the different stars, and they became like small, blinking friends above. I loved these trips outside in the cold winter air, listening to my dad narrating and explaining, while sitting on the kick sled. Still today I take delight in the stars. They tell me so much about God's greatness and plan – both in large and small settings.

I was blessed with a good father. This gave me a vital foundation so I could find faith in God as my heavenly Father later in life. A good Father who cares for me. Who patiently takes time to explain everything I don't understand myself. Who gives me time to think through and process what I don't understand. Who does not leave me alone. His hand holds me in a firm grip when life is like a journey through long, ice-cold winter nights under a dark, starless night sky.

My father held a degree in economics and business administration from Denmark and came to work in Stokmarknes, where he met and married my mother Reidun. After the wedding celebration, he and Mum stayed in her childhood home, together with my grandmother. I was born into this multi-generational family as the oldest of two siblings.

My childhood home was a big, old wooden house on the heights above the most northern town of the island, Stokmarknes. The gravel road leading up to the house had a row of spruce trees on one side. In front of the house stood a great poplar. In the last drifting snow of April, bold blue scilla and yellow, white and purple crocuses competed for attention, and through several of the bright summer months the basement wall was covered in hop flowers. On the few warm summer days we experienced, the garden was scented with the delicate fragrance of the old pink and white Alba rose trees. The lilacs had their short flowering at the end of June, with heavy white and blue blooms.

My mother was a well of creativity. She had created a fantastic flower bed by our basement door, which was bursting with small, white snowdrops and snowflakes. Behind the house we had bushes of red currant, blackcurrant, raspberries and gooseberries. We grew peas, lettuce, radish, potatoes and rhubarb in addition. Bliss was having an egg cup filled with sugar, dipping the rhubarb stalk in the sugar and munching on it with tiny baby teeth. Through long autumn evenings we would press colourful autumn leaves from maple and aspen, as we also did with small clusters of dried berries. We would also pick straw for multi-coloured Christmas cards that we made in December, bringing joy to friends and family. In my childhood almost everything was made and very little was purchased.

My mother had a small field of oats over which she kept careful watch. The grain yield was used as sheaves for the birds through the cold winter months. Every autumn Dad would put up new bird houses for starlings and flycatchers and would clean out the old ones. Great flocks of bullfinch, bohemian waxwings and great tits came to us during the winter. The large rowan tree, with its bountiful clusters of reddening berries on black, bare branches, provided food for the winged swarm. We also hung out netting bags with a mixture of lard, grain and nuts for our small, freezing, feathered friends.

At that time, it was a long way between Vesterålen and Kristiansand. If we were going to travel there, it always had to be for a longer stay. And so it became a yearly tradition to spend one summer month in Southern Norway with my dad's family. Dad could come home from his office on a Friday afternoon and announce that tomorrow was time for departure. This made my mother a world champion in quick packing of suitcases.

We belonged to a large family, and for us small northerners it was a great experience to come to Southern Norway and the cabin at Åros, to take boat trips in Blindleia, wade out on sandy river banks or just be alive, play and enjoy ourselves through lazy days with all our cousins. One of my aunts had a book with stories from many different countries, and in that book was a story of a little child who experienced a terrible rain storm, but who owned a big umbrella with bold colours. The drawing that illustrated that story was fixed on my young mind. The story came from a country called Colombia.

I also remember the excitement of sitting on my grandfather's lap when he opened his gold watch. It had two small lids that would make the sound of a pop as they sprang open. The pocket watch was usually well hidden inside the pocket of his waistcoat, underneath his jacket. We, his grandchildren, were nevertheless allowed to take turns to open the watch. It was a great thrill to get a little glimpse inside the tiny clockwork mechanism that was moving the miniscule hands around in this treasure of a pocket watch.

Grandfather's clocks were all in all really exciting. At our cabin there was also a genuine Swiss cuckoo clock. It hung high on the wall, far from the reach of small children's hands – and that was probably a good thing. In the middle of the day, when the clock was approaching twelve, there was a great throng in front of the marvel. What a miracle it was when the little wooden door would open, and the carved bird would come out and say "cuckoo, cuckoo", no less than twelve times. What a delight it was to be a child with such joy and excitement in these little things!

Ever since I was small, my interest was turned towards understanding different relationships, whether it was the silent movement of the stars or the bluish colour of the swim bladder of fish. Everything was of interest! My *why's* were many. Sometimes it came close to ending in disaster, as on that winter day when I stood at the edge of the pier and considered jumping into the sea to have a closer look at the sea urchins and star fish at the bottom of the sea, twenty metres below. Before I succeeded in putting my idea into action, I was saved and quickly taken into the office building close by. My dad worked here as the head of finance for one of the express boat companies of coastal Norway. Inside the building, I could study small ship models with considerably more safety. These ships, which were displayed in separate cases, silently sailed through long corridors, far from the dangers of the sea. Nevertheless, the dream of one day diving down into the depths of the sea never left me.

Our closest neighbours during childhood were also good friends of our family, and together with them – and the dog Sheepy – we would go on hikes. Sheepy was a lovely creature. Kind as the day is long, she would accept almost everything we kids would come up with. She would dance the waltz with my brother, and would agree to have her ears made into pigtails. Whenever she was able to collect a treat, she was immediately there with her long nose. In the summer, when the weather allowed it, we would go to the beach. And what a group we were! Our neighbours, my parents and grandmother, plus a dog and us two children. Food and beach balls were crammed into our neighbour's old Saab; only later did we get our own "Blue buck," a Volkswagen beetle of the good, old kind. Any thought that the temperature of the Arctic Ocean might be a problem, was far from our consideration as kids. We simply loved to splash around in the shallow water of that crystal clear sea that never got warmer than ten to fifteen degrees.

"We've had the best of the day," Daddy would say, as the sea fog in early afternoon came crawling down mountain clefts like clammy fingers.

However, on fishing trips, mist and rain were no hindrance. The two male members of our family were eager anglers and got plenty of lovely Arctic char and trout for many delicious Sunday dinners.

On cold autumn days, when the storm was raging and the sea was beating against the rugged coast, I could see cormorants sitting on land, stretching their wings out in order to dry them. Cormorants scared me a little. Their black feathers and hoarse cries nourished eerie images in my mind. They reminded me of spooky tales of enchanted princesses in bird's skin, and boats that would sink in stormy nights.

My imagination was well fed by the fairy tales Mum told me and my brother every Sunday. After dinner, we would find our seat on each side of my mother on the double bed; two small, expectant listeners, who were paying close attention. The fairy tales of Asbjørnsen and Moe were like a dessert digested with great enjoyment. And H.C. Andersen's stories were also popular.

Luckily there were a lot of other birds as well as the cormorants that engaged my interest. One morning we were awakened by a frantic knock on one of our basement windows. It turned out to be a seagull that wanted our attention. After knocking on the window, and in this way indicating that it wanted food, it ran out on the grass and gazed up eagerly towards the kitchen window. Pretty soon it was rewarded with bread crusts, old pieces of cheese and other delights. This seagull was named Kalle. After a few years he acquired a wife, and people who came to visit us had to be cautioned against the "bombing" from above of the highly accurate seagulls. Every summer there was a big hubbub as their young were hatched in the nest they had built in the flower bed underneath our living room window. It was amazing to see up close how the tiny gulls fought their way out of the bluish, brown speckled eggs. They received no help from their parents, but had to do it all on their own. This made them strong and well equipped to take on the many challenges life in the short summers of Nordland offered.

This childhood memory has often been helpful for me later in life. Especially when I have met people who need time to find their own solutions, without me or others who try to push our "help" on them.

But for me there were also other childhood memories. They were not only about winter fun and hot summers. Quite early a completely different reality would become part of my everyday life.

3

Toy dogs, circus curtains and being a child in hospital

When the lilacs bloom in June, I always think of the little garden at the hospital for rheumatic diseases in Oslo. It was originally a cloister garden belonging to Old Aker church. The garden lay well sheltered beneath the crown of the giant chestnut tree on the corner.

The view from Akersbakken was surrounded by low walls and wrought iron fences, lined by abundant hedges of purple lilac. There was also some basic playground equipment, and wooden benches where people could sit and enjoy themselves on warm days.

I spent a lot of time in the garden, especially when Mum had to go home and I was left alone at the hospital. It was not tolerated for children to cry here. Not even a small four year old who was afraid and lonely was allowed to cry. Already then I learned to swallow my tears. At that time the general consensus was that "good and clever children don't cry," and for me and the other young patients, it was important to be on good terms with the nurses. So when I needed to cry, I preferred to hide in one of the bathrooms of the hospital basement where no-one could find me. Especially bad was the first week after Mum left to go home again. I was so terribly home sick! I still remember how I carefully counted the blue-green tiles of the bathroom walls while the worst sobs subsided.

My problems had started with the smallpox vaccine. It had given me a huge immunological reaction when I was one year old. Sky-high fever caused swollen knees and fingers and soon led to stiffening ankles and wrists. Childhood arthritis was being discussed. I was admitted into the local hospital for observation and later moved to Oslo to the specialist hospital for rheumatic diseases. At this time it was believed that it was best for hospitalized children not to have any contact with their parents, since the little ones frequently started crying when their mother or father left them. It was not allowed for parents to stay at the hospital together with their child, and visits from home should be few and far between. There was also no financial support to allow parents to take time off work so they could be with their sick child. For me, who came from Northern Norway, this meant many and long separations from my family. In this way I became a rootless child, without belonging anywhere, with no close friends and (in time) no regular schooling. Even my dialect from Nordland vanished along the way.

Childhood arthritis was a virtually unknown concept at the time. I experienced my arms and legs being put in plaster splints, and this made me bedridden for weeks at a time. I put up with this, without a grumble. I was in a lot of pain, but I was nevertheless a patient child.

"Beate seldom complains, but she cries a lot," was written in a hospital note from this time.

When my Mum once came to take me home after a stay of several months at the hospital, she commented that the nurses in the hospital unit seemed so kind.

My response was to gently grab her hand and quietly say: "It helps that you are here!" Those words broke my Mum's heart. Perhaps she could sense something of all the things that happened that no one should know anything about.

My best friend at the hospital for rheumatism was a little wind-up dog. It had soft black fur and a red ribbon around its neck. For hours it would stroll back and forth on my bed covers as I was lying in my hospital cot. When an adult came by, my toy poodle would sometimes get to wander across the floor. I loved this small toy! It was soft to hold and gave me company when no one else was there to comfort me.

During a prayer ministry time many years later, God used the memory of this little toy. Through all the long years at the hospital a deep loneliness had been rooted in me. But God now gave me a mental image that healed me from this loneliness. In this image I saw Jesus sitting on the floor, winding up my toy dog and smiling at me. This way He showed me that I was not alone.

Through much of my childhood the hospital stays were a large part of my reality. When I turned ten, I was the first Norwegian child to be offered reconstructive surgery. Most of the joints in my body had been attacked, and dislocations were numerous and extensive, but now they would try to correct this with surgery. Slowly but surely, a number of operations were planned and carried out. With short intervals my knees, ankles and feet were being treated. Later wrists, elbows and hips were on the list.

Next to the balcony that faced the hospital garden there was a sun lounge that was being used as a monitoring unit. Following surgery I would lay there through many long nights with immense post-operative pain. In front of the large glass doors of the lounge there were child-friendly curtains. They had drawings of circus wagons, clowns and lions in cages. Sea lions with coloured balls held their silent, motionless performances in my imagination. On the curtains there was also a circus director who bore a vague resemblance to the head physician.

The pain was hard on me. The tough physical treatment to teach me to walk again, over and over again, never ended! During the short stays I had at home, I did physical exercises on the living room table every morning in order to maintain the mobility of all my joints. In addition I had to take warm pine needle baths twice a week. The baths were a good experience. Mum would sit on the bath stool and keep me company by singing and making up stories for me, accompanied by the light radiating from the copper furnace in the corner.

Not even through pain and loneliness did it cave in, the deep joy that has always been a part of me. I could rejoice over a little ladybird crawling up the hospital window. Whenever I had a bed by the window, I would always sleep with open curtains to enjoy the dawn or the beautiful starlit sky on a clear night. The window would also preferably be left open a crack so I could hear the early morning singing of birds. The squirrels who climbed up and down the chestnut tree with their chattering conversations were a great pleasure to me. Moreover there were weekend leaves and visits by my aunt, uncle and two cousins. Throughout the years, they became my second nuclear family. They were Christian, and every day they prayed for God to heal me.

But one morning when I had just turned three years old, the youngest of them, my four year old cousin, said: "I don't think God wants us to pray that Beate will be healed!"

Aunt and Uncle seemed rather shocked by what he had just said, and instantly started correcting him. But they stopped when they heard the reasoning of the eager four year old intercessor: "I think God wants us to pray that He would come to mean something special for Beate!"

And so it was! They did not stop praying that I would be healed, but in their prayers they now included a request that God would no longer be a stranger to me. Nine years later this prayer was answered.

Then a man named Jairus, a synagogue leader, came and fell at Jesus' feet, pleading with him to come to his house because his only daughter, a girl of about twelve, was dying.

As Jesus was on his way, the crowds almost crushed him. And a woman was there who had been subject to bleeding for twelve years, but no one could heal her. She came up behind him and touched the edge of his cloak, and immediately her bleeding stopped.

"Who touched me?" Jesus asked.

When they all denied it, Peter said, "Master, the people are crowding and pressing against you."

But Jesus said, "Someone touched me; I know that power has gone out from me."

Then the woman, seeing that she could not go unnoticed, came trembling and fell at his feet. In the presence of all the people, she told why she had touched him and how she had been instantly healed.

Then he said to her, "Daughter, your faith has healed you. Go in peace."

While Jesus was still speaking, someone came from the house of Jairus, the synagogue leader. "Your daughter is dead," he said. "Don't bother the teacher anymore."

Hearing this, Jesus said to Jairus, "Don't be afraid; just believe, and she will be healed."

When he arrived at the house of Jairus, he did not let anyone go in with him except Peter, John and James, and the child's father and mother.

Meanwhile, all the people were wailing and mourning for her. "Stop wailing," Jesus said. "She is not dead but asleep."

They laughed at him, knowing that she was dead.

But he took her by the hand and said, "My child, get up!"

Her spirit returned, and at once she stood up. Then Jesus told them to give her something to eat. Her parents were astonished, but he ordered them not to tell anyone what had happened.

Luke 8, 41-56

4

Jairus' daughter

I hated the "livestock shows." They were a pain and a pest to all of us patients.

These so called livestock displays were held in the auditorium of the Rheumatic Hospital. There I was quickly undressed. Busy hands lifted me up on a stool, and in this way my swollen joints and deformed knees would be put on show. Anxious, naked and frozen I stood there for public display. Over the years, countless medical students paraded past me. They touched, squeezed, and examined everything! Nothing was private. Most of the time I was allowed to keep some small panties on, but not always. I was left with a painful sense of being different, an object without value. Among other things, the result was that I lost my natural shyness.

I had turned twelve years. The recurring operations followed by intense pain, long hospital stays and separation from my family were beginning to take their toll. I had just ended my longest continuous hospitalization so far; it lasted just over eighteen months. The plans for my future were filled with countless surgical interventions. Over a few years I had been through over thirty surgical interventions for rheumatism - and that was just the beginning.

The past year I had received frequent visits from Anne Marie, a well-meaning believer, who each week prayed for me. She had given me a small, red, leather-bound New Testament which also contained the Book of Psalms. I had merely glanced through it, without understanding much of the foreign words contained in it. In addition, I owned an old Bible.

At twelve years old, I decided to end my life. Already then, I was very meticulous and calculated in all I did. I now systematically hid the painkillers and anti-inflammatory tablets they gave me at the hospital. My intuition told me that if I took all the pills at once, I would not have to wake up to any more operations. It is a sad fact that even children kill themselves. I myself was so exhausted in body and mind that I could not bear the anticipation of any more suffering. I have since come to know that the medications I had chosen as the means to commit suicide are very deadly in high doses, especially for a small child. One evening I took out my secret supply of pills.

For some reason, the old Bible had been left on the nightstand. As my gaze fell on it, a prayer was formed within me: "If you exist, God, you need to show me now! You only get this one chance!"

I grab the Bible and flip it open haphazardly. My eyes become fixed on the text in Luke 8. It is about a little girl who is also twelve years old, who has just died. Jesus had been called for, and together with his three chosen disciples and the girl's parents he enters the room where they had laid the dead body. I keep lying there and read these words about Jesus and Jairus' daughter:

> *"But he took her by the hand and said, 'My child, get up!'*
>
> *Her spirit returned, and at once she stood up. Then Jesus told them to give her something to eat."*

Spellbound, I look at the words. This must be a coincidence! A shivering goes through my inner being.

I flip through the Bible again. This time Isaiah 45 is lying open before me:

> *"I will go before you and will level the mountains. I will break down gates of bronze and cut through bars of iron.*

> *I will give you riches hidden in the darkness and treasures hidden in dark places, so you may know that I am the Lord, who has called you by name, the God of Israel.*[1]*"*
>
> *"So you may know that I am the Lord, who has called you by name, the God of Israel."*

A powerful presence fills my room, and a bright light envelops me. I close my eyes to the light, but I can still see the mighty figure who is standing before me. He has a white robe and a belt of gold. His feet are brass coloured, and his hair is long, white and looks like curly wool. His eyes are shining like fire. In one hand he holds a lampstand. He slowly comes down towards me, stands beside me and puts his other hand on my head.

I am no longer in doubt that God exists! I am filled with a deep silence and awe. Then and there I put the remains of my little life in God's hands. Death is no longer an option for me.

The next morning I throw away all the tablets. I also write to my cousin and tell him what has happened. He responds immediately by sending me a Bible reading plan for teenagers. From then on "the Bible Key" will be my companion for many years to come. At the age of twelve, I still don't know the contents of the Bible, but I later realize that the person who came to meet me there at the threshold of death was Christ Himself, as He is described in Revelation.

In the Gospel of Luke, in the story of Jairus' daughter, a woman who had been bleeding for many years is mentioned. My human spirit is on the verge of bleeding to death because of continual unseen bleeding for most of my first twelve years. But, like the woman who was healed by touching Jesus, I am saved into a new life when the Lord of Life touches me. The life that awaits me will be anything but easy. But now I know that God wants me to live, and that He will walk together with me through the difficult years. He has promised to give me "treasures hidden in dark places".

---

1 Isaiah 45, 2-3

That is a promise that will be fulfilled many times! Later I get to experience how He opens the way through impossible difficulties. Where I go, a road is repeatedly being opened before me!

5

Breathing space

When I was fifteen years old it was decided that I would be given a break from all the long hospital stays. Happy and content I embark on three years of high school in my home town. During this time I am also confirmed in the church. The countless and lengthy hospital stays had made it impossible for me to be confirmed at the usual time.

I receive good grades at school. I finish with a language bias, so after I graduate I study mathematics, physics and biology for an additional year. After this, I am able to begin my medical studies in Oslo. Now both my hips have had surgery and I have had artificial joints inserted in them. I can walk normally for the first time in many years, completely without pain or restraint. The joy over this miracle is great!

The summer before my studies begin, I visit *Revma* again. This time one of my big toes that is fixed underneath the other toes needs adjustment. It is a small procedure that requires only a few weeks of hospitalization. The pain is however exceptionally great, and after the bout I feel tired. As I have done so often at *Revma*, I spend time in the hospital chapel. It is a small, beautiful room in a quiet part deep inside the hospital, far away from the clamour of people. I often bring with me a rose or lilacs in bloom from the garden and arrange them in a small silver vase on the altar.

One evening while sitting in the quiet of the chapel, God speaks to me again: "I will give you a holiday you will never forget, but it is going to cost you tears."

What on earth can this mean? I have no holiday plans, but I am on the contrary about to begin studies at university. And what is said about tears is not sounding very cheery.

During the almost eight years that have passed since my first encounter with the Lord, I have learned this: when God speaks, one ought to listen. I also know that He only wants what is best for me. The Bible says that God collects all our tears in a bottle[2], and now I intuitively understand that something important is about to happen. I have no idea what it is, but I thank God for His great goodness towards me. Then I place all of myself in His mighty hands for all that may come to pass. As I am sitting there I am filled with silent wonder.

Two days later I get a visit from the social worker of the department. Hefinds a comfortable seat next to my bed, where I am lying with the operated foot on several large pillows. The social worker smiles at me. He then proceeds to tell me that I have been chosen as one of two patients to receive a free stay in the Canary Islands. Oslo Red Cross runs a holiday centre at Lanzarote, *Casas Heddy* (Heddy's house), and this is where a place has been prepared for me. Until then I have never been outside the borders of Norway. Now, with the words from the evening in the chapel still ringing in my ear, I wonder what might await me out there in that foreign land. I certainly have no doubt that this is the holiday God has spoken to me about.

In early August the large airplane from the north lands on the Canary sunshine island in the quivering midday heat. On black fields covered with volcanic rocks eager hands are in the process of harvesting grapes. Behind semi-circular stone fences smiling faces peek from beneath straw hats and dark headscarves. Many wave.

2 Psalm 56, 8 "Put my tears into Your bottle."

There are low, white houses flanked by flowering red and green hibiscus hedges everywhere. The air is remarkably dry and warm. I see tall palm trees on the horizon. Faced with all this I get a strange feeling of belonging here.

In Heddy's house there are many well adapted rooms for people with limited mobility. During the summer weeks I will be staying here, the centre is inhabited by disabled youth and their assistants from other Canary Islands. Many important and exciting encounters will take place here. A youth who is fluent in French gives me my first lessons in Spanish. I have learned French in high school, and this language now becomes a bridge for learning Spanish. I enjoy wonderful days in the shade of rustling palm branches. Tours are arranged to volcanic mountains and deep caves. One of the destinations is the small island of Graciosa, north of Lanzarote. Mass tourism has not yet taken over Graciosa, so the only way to get there is by a small fishing boat. The boat carves its way and thrusts ahead through the rough waters on the short but wild stretch to the island. There is also a strong current here. To go ashore, we have to stand on the gunwale and be lifted by the wrists, just as the craft is on the crest of a wave so that the gunwale is as high as the quay. Knees and elbows are scraped more than enough, but I would not have been without this experience. It is so wild here. The sandy beaches are huge and solitary, the sea is azure blue, and seagulls dive into the sea. In the distance the cliffs of Lanzarote lie as a dark frame behind this summer image. God has indeed given me a holiday I will not forget! Some years will still pass before I understand how the tears that were announced will come into play.

As the holiday came to an end, I was asked if I would consider coming back the following summer as a volunteer. The answer was given without hesitation. Through many summers I will return to *Casas Heddy*. Later I will also become familiar with the other Canary Islands, and I develop many close friendships with people here. One of these friends is Rafa, with whom I work as a volunteer.

Back in Norway my days are filled with studies. They are interesting, but demanding years. Challenges queue up. How should I for example get to the autopsy hall on the fourth floor of the Anatomical Institute? The solution is found in using the so-called *morgue lift*. Fortunately I feel very alive!

A spiritual breathing space during this time is provided by activities with *Guds fred* (God's peace) in Oslo. This is a group that offers Bible nights, conversations and social welfare on the streets. Once a month gospel nights are held in the large Church of the Holy Trinity in the middle of the city. I quickly become engaged in work among Spanish speaking refugees and immigrants. Many of them struggle with the new and in many ways frigid Norwegian daily life. I am not aware of this then, but both the summers at Lanzarote, where I learn Spanish among other things, and the Christian work among refugees from the south, will give me a valuable foundation for later years in South America.

6

Bright spots

I truly enjoy my time as a medical student! Years fly by at a fast pace, and I am able to keep up. Only the last year turns out differently. Because one of the inserted hips becomes loose, I am forced to take an extended break from studies. With a broken femur I end up in bed for several months. My sorrow is great. My student friends have thankfully not forgotten me, and they come regularly for visits. They show up in flocks, occasionally in white medical coats, other times just as friends in regular clothing. The nurses do not quite know how to deal with this growing crowd of visitors who show up at all hours. Some of those who pay me a visit are doing their internship at the hospital, and cannot easily be dismissed.

Unfortunately complications arise in the hip and I have to go through several surgical procedures – again! Will it never end? The questions that bubble up inside my tired soul are many and painful.

As often is the case at the hospital, finding a place where I can be by myself is difficult. I choose the bathroom, which is mostly vacant in the daytime. One morning I pour out my heart in prayer: "Lord, help me find a meaning in all these difficult things happening!"

When I come out into the corridor again I hear a loud gasp from one of the neighbouring rooms. Grete is lying there stretched out in bed. For many years Grete and I belonged to the same Christian fellowship, but now we have not seen each other in years. As I pass by the open door to her room she has however recognized me.

Her life is in ruins. Just like me Grete is experiencing a crisis. She has been hit hard by a ruthless bout of arthritis, and the side effect of the medication she has to take has given her as many as twenty-two fractures of the spine. Subsequently some well-meaning souls have brought her to a "healing service." She is brought into the church on a stretcher, but instead of showing her compassion she is met with accusations that she has sinned. These sins have, according to the pastors, brought on Grete's serious illness. And as if that is not enough, her husband wants to divorce her. He is apparently unable to handle more illness and has found a new, healthy woman.

Grete is completely broken in body and soul. Tears are slowly flowing down her sunken cheeks. This morning she has prayed desperately to a God she almost does not believe in anymore: "God, if you exist, I ask that you send Beate my way! She also has arthritis, but in spite of the disease she believes in you. I need to share my pain with someone who can understand my own. If you give me this miracle, God, I will believe in you."

So it was maybe not so surprising that Grete lets out a cry as she sees me passing by outside in the corridor.

Together we cry and pray that God will intervene in Grete's life. I know with myself how difficult it is to hold on and continue when everything is black, and not a single star is visible on the inner heaven.

As Grete and I meet again, we have both received answers to prayer. God has shown me a meaning in all that is meaningless. It is enough. This becomes a powerful testimony and in many ways a turning point for both of us. It lets us know that God sees, that He cares, and that no obstacle is too hard for Him to overcome. Slowly Grete and I move forward, into each of our daily lives. Times ahead of us may not always be easy to deal with, but God is never distant from us small ones who have taken our refuge in the mighty God of Israel.

Grete will after a while receive her good health back. For me it will at times be quite different.

Being a bulb in the hand of God

I am sitting by the window. The garden outside the hospital window is covered with a blanket of leaves. Trees stretch their black, naked branches towards the pale November sky. The branches are like hands in a frozen scream.

The blazing disk of the sun is about to disappear below the horizon. A short day is over, and an emerging redness on the western sky slowly wipes out the last shimmer of day in the cold twilight.

It is autumn. In a little while the wilting leaves will be covered by a thick layer of snow. Everything will grow silent. Without life. As dead.

But just a few days ago I planted spring bulbs outside in the garden. They are like small grey mute lumps. They seem to have neither life nor colour. They are like small insignificant good-for-nothings that have been stuffed deep into the dark earth, as if they have been forgotten by God and by people.

But then, one spring day, those little bulbs of mine have been transformed into beautiful flowers. With an inborn assurance they stick their heads above the soil, often while the snow still lies in piles here. They know that spring is coming! A spring full of light, life and colours. A spring they are created to be a part of.

Sometimes I feel like such a small bulb, buried and forgotten in a darkness that can seem infinite and all-encompassing. But because I believe no darkness is too dark to be lit up by God's care, and no darkness is too dark for our Lord to use it to serve His purposes, I have hope! My hibernation is accompanied by the assurance that spring will come one day. For it is in precisely this that God shows His love. He lets the apparent death process in darkness become the source of a brand new joy. Of a brand new life. Of a completely new and colourful existence that arises out of the ruins of autumn darkness and winter cold. In the small bulbs, as in me, the Lord has laid down attributes and possibilities that cannot grow or come to life unless a time of silence in deepest darkness is lived through. God lets His creatures live through times of autumn and winter not to break them down or torment them, but to perfect His work.

I can imagine the small bulbs in the soil as if they were sleeping, trusting children, surrounded by safe, caring hands. God truly watches over His little ones! Like them, I will live through my own autumn storms and winter slumbers while I, with hope in my heart, wait for the fulfilment of God's great promises.

It is easy to forget that if darkness did not exist, I would not be able to rejoice in the light.

That one twilight in November shows me that the strength and power of the sun's rays may cease for a night. But it will surely return, this time with the warm, optimistic rays of the morning sun that will cause the shadows of night to flee!

Lord, grant me the courage to let the silent, optimistic waiting of the bulb be mine! Hide me in your hands, Lord, while the winter storms of my life rage outside! Sing to my heart about the spring you know will come! Amen.

7

An important encounter and an actual miracle

As a newly qualified doctor I am lucky enough to spend my whole internship in Bærum (close to Oslo). Thus I am spared from difficult moving. The health centre I eventually become associated with has around the clock responsibility for Fornebu International Airport, which is close by. After a while the police understand that the centre has a Spanish speaking doctor, something they make use of at various times.

One day two huge policemen come dragging a thin, dark-haired young woman along with them. As she drops down on the chair in front of my desk, she is obviously terrified. Not all our new citizens come to Norway with the experience that policemen can be trusted.

Outside it is freezing Norwegian winter, and the snow is falling. The woman stares blankly at the icy windowpane. She has neither passport nor other documents that can say who she is. The police are however under the impression that she speaks Spanish. Now she is sitting in front of me, shaking. The eyes that meet mine are large and scared. She does not understand a single word of Norwegian or English.

I present myself in Spanish. With the same language I also promise that nothing of what she tells me will be used against her. Moreover, I tell her that she will not be arrested. When the police brought her here to the health centre, it is because they have understood that she needs help.

When she hears her native language, she starts crying. She is shaking with stifled sobs, which finally decrease slightly. The appointments I have for the rest of the day are cancelled. The woman in front of me gets the time she so desperately needs.

It turns out that she is a refugee from a country in Latin America. Her husband has been put to death. She has herself been tortured so that she miscarried and lost their only child. She has been a teacher in her home country, and she and her husband were both members of the banned union. After intense interrogations, she was released, and eventually managed to flee the country. All her savings were used up on the flight. After she escaped, she heard that her aging parents were also being brought in for questioning.

Through fragments of Spanish words and phrases I get a glimpse into a foreign, terrifying existence. The story continues, now dealing with what happens as she crosses into the neighbouring country. There the woman is taken in by an international humanitarian aid organization. And after some long months she has thus ended up here in Norway, this winter country in the far north.

She is a forlorn, frightened woman with considerable external and internal wounds. Only slowly is she able to adapt to a new and foreign society. Like so many of those who have come here she will never quite settle into our society. The longing for what was, always remains. In Norway awaits a safe, but in many ways lonely, life.

The story of this woman is not unique. Many refugees and asylum seekers resemble her. However, this woman and her destiny is my first encounter with the ice-cold cruelty of humanity. Later in life, when the violence of another country has crossed my path, I will often think back upon this encounter which I have never quite forgotten.

*

One day during my internship as a doctor I suddenly start coughing. I develop a fever and after some time my skin turns intensely yellow. My weight spirals down, and I feel increasingly dizzy. Finally, I am unable to stay on my feet, let alone work. I am admitted for further examination. It is determined that I have haemolytic anaemia. Antibodies bind themselves to red blood cells, which are then quickly destroyed. The bone marrow tries to compensate by producing ever increasing numbers of red blood cells, but eventually collapses because of the violent overproduction.

It is a beautiful autumn day when the chief physician comes to speak to me about this. In clear words he tells me that it is too late for me. Everything that can be done, has been done. The only thing that can save my life now is a miracle. In plain language he explains that the time has come when I must prepare to die. I am told that the hospital willingly will help me get in contact with a priest.

Dean Torgeir Havgar comes to visit me from Gamle Aker Church. His son and their family are good friends of mine, and he has heard a rumour that there is something wrong. I am already so weak that I am unable to speak clearly. Simply turning in bed gives me terrible heart palpitations. I sleep away more and more hours of the day.

The following day, which is a Saturday, Mrs Havgar comes to pick me up. I am piled into a wheelchair, pushed across the road and into the old medieval church. It is always good to come here. In here I feel like one of many who have gone before me. Now the dean is dressed in full regalia and has placed himself behind the old altar. This will be done properly! He has even written his own small liturgy for the occasion.

The three of us celebrate communion together in the large, silent church. Afterwards the dean prays for me and anoints me with oil.

> *Is anyone among you suffering? Let him pray. Is anyone cheerful? Let him sing psalms. Is anyone among you sick? Let him call for*

the elders of the church, and let them pray over him, anointing him with oil in the name of the Lord. And the prayer of faith will save the sick, and the Lord will raise him up. And if he has committed sins, he will be forgiven.[3]

With simple words Dean Havgar commits my life into God's hands and prays that the Lord of Life will touch me. I am personally exhausted, but at the same time filled with a deep peace.

The next day one of the nurses points out that I have flushed, rosy cheeks. The following day, which is Monday, my blood samples show that the haemoglobin value has gone up twenty per cent since the last test on Friday. Five days later my blood levels have increased by a whole sixty per cent. Dean Havgar seems as overwhelmed as me. Even the most unbelieving of the medical staff has difficulty explaining away this physically proven miracle. For me there is no doubt: God has really done a miracle.

This miracle did not come slowly, but very quickly. It fills me with a holy wonder and a quiet joy for a long time. A few weeks later I am back in full time work again.

3 James 5, 13-15

8

A doctor's calling

As a new doctor I visit various medical fields until I find what will become my specialty. First I gain experience in such diverse fields as ophthalmology (eye diseases) and pain research. But it is in adult psychiatry that I will find my final place.

When I get there it is already after a few years of pain research. Through my profession, I have been to Iceland and Australia, USA and Denmark. I have learned important lessons about how children communicate pain. One research project is completed and my first scholarly article published. I am at the same time engaged in Christian counselling, and receive teaching through *Helhet gjennom Kristus* (Victorious Ministry through Christ). This gives me valuable experience both in Norway and Sweden.

Then one day I end up at Prestesæter Psychiatric Hospital at Toten. I do not plan to work here very long, because my advisors at *Rikshospitalet* (the national hospital) in Oslo want me to join a new, comprehensive research project there. This will however not happen. I enjoy my work at Prestesæters section 1B very much, and my boss is rubbing his hands and loudly proclaiming that he will succeed in recruiting me to adult psychiatry. He will get his way, but then a completely different "boss" intervenes. It happens on a dark winter night.

As the on call doctor, I have visited the psychiatric emergency unit in connection with an admission. As I am driving back to the apartment where I live, I see a small group of people who are walking in front of me on the road. It is a group of patients together with a nurse who is taking an evening walk outside in the cold night. One of the patients turns and looks toward my car. I know who he is; he is a brute of a man who can sometimes be violent. However, this night his eyes are filled with uncertainty. In the light of the car all I see is a small, scared child. The large, frightened eyes make me think of an animal pursued by hunters.

I will never forget what happens next. I am all alone in the car when I hear the Lord ask me a simple question:

"Beate, can you leave these my little ones?"

Those who walk in front of me on the road are not exactly small – some of them are more than six feet tall – but I understand what God is telling me. Behind their tough exterior is hidden a personality with one or more vulnerable elements – pieces that seem so tiny, as if they belong to a child. Many of them are quite lonely, perhaps shunned by family and friends.

This night I dedicate myself and my life to serve God as a psychiatrist for adults and as a counsellor for people with shattered souls. This is how I start a journey that will prove to be very demanding and cost my all. I understand that God loves these people infinitely and feels a deep pain over their great suffering. I also realize that He wants me to be there for Him, as His hands, ears, eyes and mouth in the face of this enormous suffering. They live with an inner being that has been shattered into a thousand pieces, but God can, with me as one of His tools, meet each individual and do something with the parts of their lives that are broken. No one can help everyone, least of all me, but even though I am only a small, physically frail person, I believe that I can help someone with God's support and help.

This is the way I make my real entry into adult psychiatry. Many years will come and go before I one day experience something that will change my life forever. I eventually work as chief physician at one of the major psychiatric hospitals in Oslo.

My office is not located inside the unit, and one of the patients who has an appointment with me, runs ahead of the nurse. This person also manages to push me down the stairs. I am able to stop myself from falling all the way down the long concrete staircase, but the physical damage is still substantial. One hip prosthesis has penetrated through my pelvic bone. Once again I end up at the now so familiar operating table. Many in the unit where I work become victims of similar and even more serious injuries. In three months there are fifty-seven personal injuries in my unit.

Through these difficult days I receive good support from my friend and colleague Jasiu. He is a refugee who has come to Norway from the east. He accomplishes what no other anaesthesiologist before him has, making sure that I experience hardly any postoperative pain.

Through our research work Jasiu and I have had considerable contact and have come to know each other well. For hours we can discuss medical research, literature and faith. Jasiu is also a Christian.

When the day of another scheduled operation is at hand, I often feel afraid. The night before there is showering, enema and body parts that need to be shaved. During a private moment in the cool bathroom my hand pats the area that will be operated on the next day. Starting tomorrow, a new scar will be mine. Once again I will lose a part of myself. Every time I live through a loss.

As the morning starts at daybreak in the anaesthesia room, Jasiu is by my side. He is like a safe and steadfast image of the presence of Christ. We pray together, before he injects the anaesthetic into my trembling hand.

"Lord," I pray, "give wisdom to everyone who is involved in today's procedure!

I believe in your love for me, and I commit myself into your hands. Whether I live or die, I belong to you!"

So far I have been through one hundred and three 'rheumatic' surgical interventions. I always wake up after the anaesthetic!

I have been at death's door many times, but always come crawling back to life.

The day after an operation my aunt Bergliot usually comes visiting. She is silently sitting by my bed while praying. Sometimes she reads a verse from the Bible, but first and foremost she is just present with me in my pain.

Aunt believes that I am like a cork: even though I am pushed far down in the water glass of life, I always float back up to the surface. She may be right. God has given me an unquenchable will to live that takes me through it all. It may take time and it is not always easy, but I always get back up and move forward.

So also this time. When I return to my position as chief physician of the unit, the patient who pushed me down the stairs says: "Imagine that you are so fond of me that you dare to come back!"

They are perhaps minor words, but they convey a profound truth. I have been severely damaged, but I have no thought of giving up what I consider my life calling.

But then I am injured again. A young man, who is well known to the unit, has recently been admitted. He is hallucinating and says that he sees dark figures in the corners. A voice says that he must kill me, because I am allegedly dangerous. So he tries to strangle me and seriously scratches my skin. Help comes quickly as my security alarm is triggered, but in a way it is too late. I have bleeding wounds on my hands and end up with a high fever. It turns out that I have been infected with a severe sepsis of gut bacteria which was hidden under the fingernails of this man. Over the next two years I am regularly tested for possible HIV or Hepatitis C infection.

The infection spreads to the last operated hip and will be impossible to overcome. For more than two years I toil through constant antibiotics and operations to close the exuding tract that repeatedly opens up between the hip joint and skin. Throughout this time I am in full time work, but must eventually throw in the towel and go on long-term sick leave.

At last I get the message that the hip prosthesis needs to be removed, and that it may not be possible to insert a new joint there. I will most likely end up in a wheelchair.

A hope is slowly shattered – the hope of being able to walk normally, to be able to run on the beach underneath a warm sunny sky while the waves caress my bare feet. I grieve.

9

In the dark valley

Then it arrives, the dreaded day. It is September 1st 1998, and I am once again wheeled into the operating theatre. I know little of what awaits me.

This time it goes wrong. During the introduction of the anaesthetic I have spasms in the larynx and stop breathing. Four minutes pass, my lungs are about to collapse, but with a gasp I draw breath again. Oxygen-rich air flows to my lungs again. But the damage has been done. The high pulse and the dangerously increasing blood pressure in a body that is desperately fighting against death cause a bleeding of the spinal cord. I am unaware of it then, but will soon wake up, paralyzed from the neck down.

While I am still completely unconscious, I experience walking through a river of green, cascading water. There is nothing hindering me from moving anymore and my body seems almost transparent. I slowly come out of the water and onto a beach, helped by benevolent souls that resemble me.

Then I see Him. I recognize Him by the oval nail marks through each of His wrists. It is Jesus. He takes my hands in His and says:

"So, you have come, Beate!"

A deep compassion flows towards me.

"Yes, Lord. But I am so tremendously tired –"

It is as if a stream of invisible water is flowing over me. Little by little the unsettling weariness washes away.

Afterwards a long conversation between me and Jesus follows. Later I will not remember the details of this conversation, but I have a lingering sense that we are speaking about the future there on the riverbank, although today I cannot say for sure.

Finally Jesus looks at me again and asks: "Do you want to stay here or do you want to go back?"

It is as if He has asked me if I want strawberry or chocolate ice-cream. I know intuitively that He loves me just the same whether I stay here or return to life.

"If you will, Lord, I will return," and begin to make my way towards the green river again.

The next moment I wake up to unbearable pain. I am paralyzed from the neck down, and my body burns as if thousands of irons are passing back and forth over me. I am extremely dizzy and can hardly speak. I have no strength to move, and am not even able to lift a hand. So I cry and scream that I want to return to Jesus on the beach!

Some nurses come running to my side. They tell me that my neck is very swollen, and that I should not cry. If I do, I may be strangled. I must be strong now, I am told. Faintly over there in the distance I notice Jasiu's sad eyes. I realize that something has gone very, very wrong.

For three weeks I battle with death. But I survive. All my loved ones come to visit. Almost all. Only Rafa is too far away to come. The others stand around my bed, gazing at me helplessly. They would gladly help me, but nothing can be done about the physical and medical condition. But many pray.

My pains are terrible. Only slowly will the damaged nerve tissue calm down within me. My legs are hidden under some kind of cage to prevent the duvet from touching my skin and triggering spasms.

This is a dark valley. I spend the next eleven months on my back in a sickbed. I feel very alone with all my difficult thoughts.

A bruised reed he will

not break,

and a smouldering wick he will

not snuff out.

In faithfulness he will bring forth justice;

Isaiah 42, 3

10

Loss

As waves on rough seas the physical pain washes over me. Day and night. Over and over again. I cannot sleep.

Only after several months have I become stable enough to be taken into the hospital swimming pool. From the bed I am pulled over on to a metal bench and lowered into the warm water. Three people need to support me to keep me from turning over. The enormous pain and insomnia has made my metabolism go crazy. My entire body has thus swelled up, and my weight has increased by 90 pounds. I feel like a hippo, and avoid looking at myself in the mirror.

Paralyzed from the neck down, I find that I nevertheless can move my legs a little bit in the pool: one step today, two tomorrow. Even though you are paralyzed, it does not always mean that you have lost feeling. Two different parts of the nervous system control movement and sensation. I still have very little sensation of the skin, and have no balance. I am eventually able to move a bit by myself in the warm water, without too much pain. Also my hands slowly come back to life. Well supported by pillows as I lie on my back in the bed, I am able to cross stich through long, waking nights. A practical book rack also makes it possible for me to read.

A Spanish friend, Belinda, agrees to train me in Spanish grammar. She is a huge blessing as she faithfully shows up every week with linguistic challenges for me. This is good for me, as it helps me keep the faith that one day I will be able to get up and move on. That there is a way out of the valley of lost opportunities. I have still not lost courage. I am like an ant trying to knock an elephant down to the ground, refusing to admit that I do not have a chance.

Rafa calls and wants to come for a visit. He has been here before, but this time I say no. I cannot bear the thought of him seeing me the way I have become. I want him to remember me as I was before. However, I commit a terrible mistake by keeping him away from my pain. For fear of losing him, I reject him.

Rafa and I met at Lanzarote, where we worked as volunteers for groups of disabled Spanish. Shoulder by shoulder we worked from morning till evening. We were both medical workers. Rafa was from the Canary Islands. We enjoyed each other's company a lot. In the years that followed we would keep in touch despite the great distance between Norway and Gran Canaria. We met as often as we could, and had many of the same interests. Long letters frequently crossed the Atlantic. Through several years a deep friendship had developed. The plan was that I would complete further education in psychotherapy, and later move to Gran Canaria. I was already approved as a psychiatrist and had been granted a licence as a Spanish doctor. I had been welcomed with open arms by the local Medical Association. According to the plan I would complete one year of training at a large psychiatric hospital outside Las Palmas on Gran Canaria, before becoming the chief physician of a psychiatric clinic in one of the small towns in the north of Gran Canaria. I had even bought a small apartment there, which was in the process of being renovated. Life was smiling at me from all sides – until September 1st 1998.

On September 1st in the evening, while I lie in recovery at the post-operative unit, Rafa calls and asks how the operation has gone. That night something shatters inside him too. He has always struggled with goodbyes, and now it dawns on him that my chances of making it are slim. The charge nurse in intensive care explains to him that the major blood loss, paralysis and numerous fractures of the femur do not bode well. In addition, the extensive paralysis gives me respiratory problems. Slowly Rafa begins to prepare for an inevitable farewell. Poor Rafa! He is so very far away.

Finally I have to tell him that I cannot start in my planned position as a psychiatrist at Gran Canaria. It happens over the phone. Rafa turns completely silent. His silence resounds on the phone for many long minutes. Once again something shatters to pieces. When he is able to speak again, his voice has a bitter sound. His pain has also become too great.

He is not the only one to disappear. Many colleagues and friends in the academic community rarely or never contact me again. I seem to have resigned my membership of everything I was recently a part of.

I am no longer able to take care of myself. Through the years that follow a number of good helpers – personal assistants – will march through my life. They are good people, and most of them are skilled at their job. This is without doubt the best solution for me. This is the only way I can continue to live at home.

During a transitional period I will visit several rehabilitation centres at home and abroad. I will, however, never be able to walk normally again. Helped by shoulder high crutches I am sometimes able to walk a few metres. That is it. From here onwards a wheelchair goes for me.

People who end up in a wheelchair lose something of themselves. In a subtle way, independence is affected. From now on I am dependent on other people to manage even the most everyday tasks such as cooking and getting dressed. The ability to decide when I want to do what becomes limited. I am also always in need of more help than is being offered. The wheelchair becomes a barrier against closeness with other people. This is anyway how it is for me in the beginning of my life as a "quad".

Losses are great and many. Not only have I lost my physical ability, but also much of what until now was a part of my life. Nothing remains the way it was. All uncried tears freeze to snowflakes that slowly descend and hide the torn landscape of my heart. However, the pain lies there as a slowly growing glacier, distant, untouched and icy.

11

When what is frozen melts – God's solutions

These are difficult times for me. Everything has to be learned again.

One day the surgeon explains to me that it is unrealistic to believe that I will ever be able to go back to work as a psychiatrist. Then a dam bursts inside of me. For three days I sit in my special chair crying. A sea of disappointment and loss reaches the surface of my exhausted mind. And so it finds its way out, through the many tears that until now have not been shed. Where I sit, I no longer have to be strong.

Then it is that Jesus comes. Suddenly He is standing there next to me. He looks at me with gentle, compassionate eyes. I think He knows what I am thinking: If I had known what would await me the day I said yes to go back to life, I would have chosen to stay with Him. Now He is asking another question of me:

"Beate, do you remember what you did the night before your last medical exam?"

Of course I remember it! After clearing my study space of all my books and the teacup, binders and postcards, I stopped my car outside a white brick church in downtown Oslo. I found the church door ajar and walked inside. On the wall of the quiet sanctuary there hung a large crucifix. I stopped in front of the crucifix, and surrendered my medical profession to God.

Where I am now sitting in the wheelchair, the Lord speaks to me again: "Give the broken pieces of your medical profession to me!"

I burst into sobs. Finally I nevertheless manage to do what He had asked of me. In prayer I give the broken pieces of my life to Him. He gets them one by one – my crushed expectations, my future as someone on a disability allowance, all the plans and projects that will never happen.

When my crying finally dies down, I am filled with a deep, inexplicable peace. I know that God has accepted my offering.

After a few days I manage to resign my position as chief physician and hand over research projects to others. Then I call Spain and decline the offer that is still open for me there. I know that I will not be able to meet their needs in a wheelchair.

Gradually my sick leave turns into disability pension. These are strange times!

Three months later I get a letter from Colombia. A Colombian pastor and his wife, whom I met in Portugal many years ago, have returned to their native Colombia. I got to know them in 1991 while visiting my cousin with family, who were missionaries together with them in Portugal. In Colombia this pastor's hometown Armenia has been devastated by a massive earthquake that has killed thousands. Others have survived, but are reduced to poverty. Many have life-changing injuries. In their letter they tell me that God has spoken to them that Armenia needs Christian psychologists and psychiatrists. So they ask: Can I come on a short visit?

Suddenly it is as if a bunch of butterflies is released in my stomach. A bubbling joy is pressing to the point that I start laughing.

What in the world is happening?

I am completely bewildered. How can an earthquake in Colombia pertain to me, stuck in a wheelchair? If I am completely honest, I think I have dealt with enough "earthquakes" in my own life. The only thing I look forward to now is to return to the Canary

Islands and enjoy my new apartment which will be ready in a few months. A ramp has been placed between the living room and kitchen, and the front door has been moved so that I can enter with a wheelchair. Master builder Manolo and carpenter Antonio are doing a fantastic job with the apartment! Two years have passed since the difficult September day when life as I knew it ended. I have slowly started to accept my new life. With the joyful expectation of a child I look forward to returning to Gran Canaria!

BENEATH A BLUE GUAYACÁN

Everyone knows that guayacáns have yellow
blossoms.
Only my guayacán is blue.
It has the colour of a tropical sky
arching above the blazing day.
It is deep blue as the oceans deep,
where seven different shades of blue
wash away all sounds from the surface.
It is blue as the lonely sorrow of dark night hours.
It is blue as the sparkling joy of being alive.

Beate before her
journey to Colombia.

Together with her mother at her baptism, February 1958.

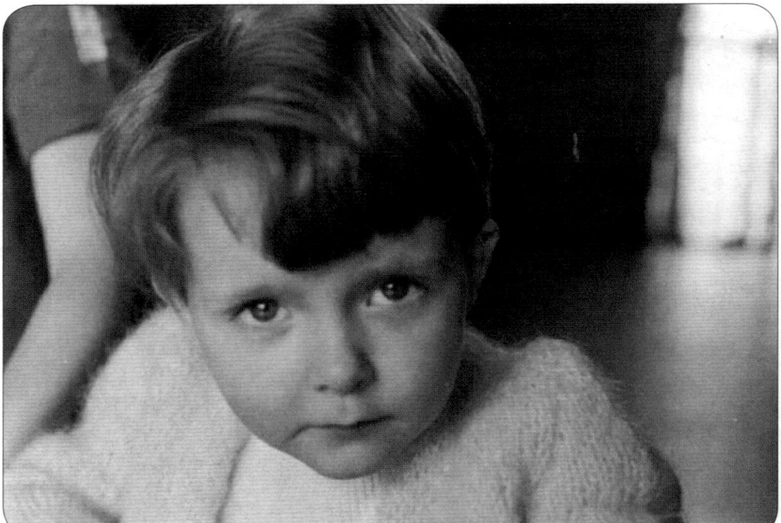

About 4 years old. Small and alone in hospital.

About 5 years old. A child's birthday at the Rheumatic Hospital. Beate is standing at the back.

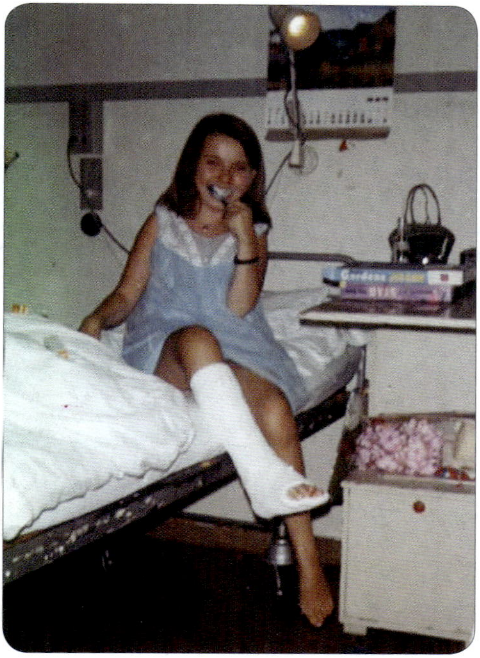

12 years old with newly operated ankle. The cast was on for 3 months.

Beate is reading her Bible just before one of her operations at the Rheumatic Hospital during the 1990s – an operation that would alter her life.

Colombia, and the city of Armenia, would become the place of Beate's work.

Armenia city centre. Both rich and poor live here.

Together with her personal assistant Griselda.

Volunteering at the rehab centre in Colombia in 2003.

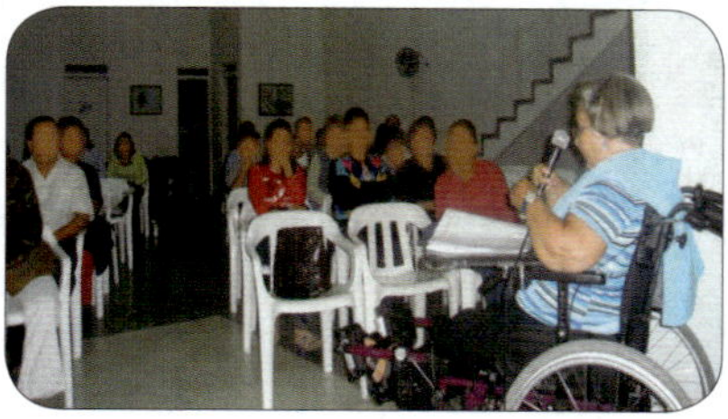

Beate teaching in Colombia.

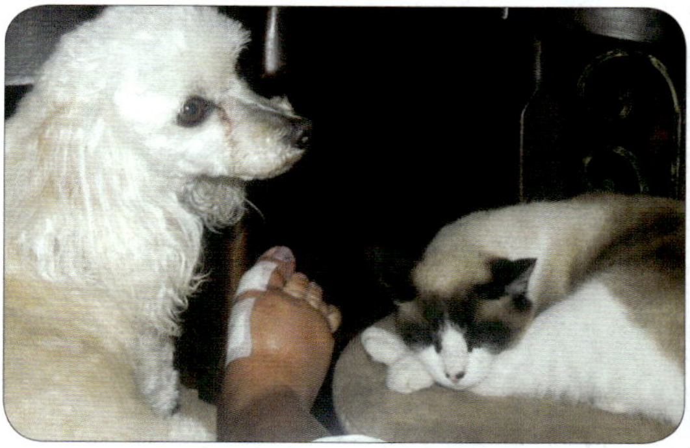

Lucas and Pixi

Saturnino, the cat

Beate diving

The Cocora Valley

El Caimo, a beautiful place to live.

12

Spring

Through the hazy heat Gran Canaria comes into view far below. Soon the plane will land.

My good old friends are there with warm words and welcoming hugs. My assistant and I are given accommodation with a neighbour while the renovation of my apartment is being completed.

It is full spring. During the winter there was snow in the mountains, we are told. Now the almond trees stand in full blossom, like a sea of white and pink on a green background. An ancient cross stands between tall pines. I go there to give the rest of my life to Jesus, and to let go of burdens that have become too heavy to bear. The wind rustles through the pine forest and carries with it my silent screams. By the foot of the cross a lone poppy waves gently in the wind.

Sometimes when the evening concert of the frogs begins, accompanied by the song of cicadas, I close my eyes and remember: the sparkling stars on a dark night sky – a deep peace – a feeling of belonging. That was before the time of great sorrow. Darkness is still filled by the hoarse songs of shearwater birds as they fly through the night. Waves crash as before against the cliffs by the lighthouse. The sun sinks into the sea in a splendour of gold, pink and turquoise behind the mighty chest of the Teide volcano, and the night slowly creeps in over the neighbouring island to the west.

Surges of pain flow through my mind, so great and deep is the cup of pain.

Many years earlier Rafa and I are on one of our many Sunday trips to the central mountains of Gran Canaria. The almond trees were a sight and we stopped to take pictures. A woman, who grafted trees, gave us an armful of flowering almond tree branches. After the trip we placed the branches in the vase on the floor in front of the mirror, and for many days the house was filled with the fresh scent of almond blossoms. An image of happiness? Pink and white flowers on a dark background. I have returned to Gran Canaria and a few days ago the Lord reminded me of this event. It is as if He wants to show me that the symbol of the "watching tree" was given as a gift already then.

In spring the almond tree is the first tree to bloom and it blooms on bare branches.

"What do you see, Jeremiah?" the Lord asked.[4]

"I see a branch of a watching tree," Jeremiah answers about the almond tree.

"You have seen correctly," the Lord answered. "I am vigilantly watching to see that my words and promises are fulfilled."[5]

The Lord watches over the fulfilment of His word in my life also!

4 Jeremiah 1, 11-12, rendered freely by the author.

5 God replies with a word sounding very similar to "almond" that means "watching" in Hebrew.

Lord!
Have mercy on me!
I am so very tired.
You know me,
You know everything that is stirring in my heart.
My yearning is as fragile almond flowers
on the dark branches of the night.
I believe in Your love for me!
Help me to wait, together with You,
underneath the almond tree!
Help me to have courage to move forward,
together with You!
And when darkness envelops me,
help me to not lose my footing,
but to trust that You who walk together with me,
turn night to light!

Amen.

13

Calling

It is a quivering hot day in June and I am sitting at the pier in the harbour. I am still on Gran Canaria, and the colourful fishing boats are just in after collecting the night's catch in the round squid pots. One of the boats with the name "Beatriz" written on the bow is pulled up on shore. I smile because that is the name they call me here. Beatriz.

This day is important. This afternoon my apartment will be ready and Manolo the builder has promised to bring me the keys. I will finally have time for myself.

Over the last few months I have little by little bought all the necessary furniture and equipment which is now in place at the apartment. I now look forward to occupying my own home. A dream is starting to come true.

Then with a beep I receive an incoming text message: "Call Norway! Colombia has called! They want you to come!"

Half conscious I call the familiar number of Tone, my cousin's wife. She has just received a call from the pastors in Armenia, Colombia. I have been invited to come to the dedication of a new small rehabilitation centre for disabled children.

The centre will be run by people from the couple's church, and they wonder if I can come and help them get started. They know I am no longer able to walk, but that is not a problem they say. Quite on the contrary, they believe God wants me to go there.

I am crying, so confused am I. My assistant Anne-Maija is crying too. She has followed me through the last years of horror and knows what the opportunity of having my own "little shelter" in the form of an apartment on Gran Canaria means to me, despite the fact that I will not be able to work as planned. For so many years I have been looking forward to this day, with my own home on the island. But I will not get to stay here? What is this about?

Suddenly I become aware of my surroundings. I am sitting right in front of the monument erected at the place from which Christopher Columbus embarked in 1492 before sailing the long way across the sea to the New World. At once I feel Jesus' presence. This time I don't see him, I just know that He is there beside me.

"Beate," he says, "what will you do now?"

Slowly it dawns on me what I will answer. It comes as a crystal clear thought: "If I don't go to Colombia, I will always wonder what would have happened if I did!"

I look at the fishing boat "Beatriz" lying ashore right beside me. I realize that I am also about to pull my life's little boat up on shore – to follow the Lord to Colombia, far away from the spring and flowering of the Canary Island.

This is how I end up heading across the Atlantic a few months later together with my personal assistant. After a stopover in Caracas in Venezuela the plane climbs up alongside high mountains before a while later descending down and landing in Colombia's capital Bogotá. I am sitting by the window glancing out. Some of the high mountains below us are covered with snow. The sunset colours the entire landscape in a pinkish orange.

But I am sure I have seen this image before! Suddenly I recognize the dream landscape that has followed me for so many years. However, now it is real. It is here, right now, beneath the plane! Slowly my eyes are filled with tears – this time because of thankfulness to the Lord who watches over what He has said. And for Him nothing is impossible!

The plane comes down for landing. I gaze out on yellow plantations and blushing fields, filled with roses. It is a mighty sight.

On the ground we are greeted by reliable people who just wish us the best. The thin air makes me a little dizzy and gives me a headache like a helmet. I have a bit of altitude sickness, *soroche,* as they call it here. Soon I am allowed to find rest among white, starched linen sheets. A bouquet of yellow, fragrant roses is standing on the nightstand.

The journey continues towards Armenia the next day, a city in the heart of Colombia. In the vibrating machine of a small plane we dance through turbulence over the sky-high tops of the Andes Mountains. When the plane has landed and the door goes up I see them – the strange trees along the runway. They look like naked umbrellas, and I smile to myself. Of course they are here, they too, the trees from the other dream! One of the workers at the airport tells me that the trees are guayacáns, a variety of acacia tree only found on the high plains of Latin America. They grow in arid ground and are incredibly strong. In ancient times this wood was worth more than pure gold. There are fewer guayacáns now, because the particular birds that spread the seeds of the tree are nearly extinct. When guayacáns are cut down a reddish heart appears in the middle of the trunk. Everything matches my dream, down to the tiniest detail! I cannot be in doubt for a moment. I have come here because God Himself wants it! He has a plan with my little life that has been shattered to pieces. When I eventually dive in with culture shock like a belly flop, it will be important for me to remember this moment.

For a Northerner like me the heat in Armenia is fierce. When we left Norway we had a temperature of twenty-seven degrees below zero and the sound of snow crackling under our feet and wheels. In Armenia the thermometer shows thirty-two degrees of heat! Humidity is almost at a hundred per cent, so I gasp for air and wonder if I can survive here. When it is raining, and it does so frequently, it is like standing in a hot shower.

The day after arrival we go to the new rehabilitation centre, where I will volunteer for several years. Everything else from my dreams of many years is there – the children with crooked eyes, the white houses and shady trees. One day the last thing will also fall into place. It happens when one of the physiotherapists brings out two large balls, a red and a green.

14

Encounters

At the centre I receive my own small office. We call it the butterfly workshop. It is an important name as it speaks of how all of us have an opportunity to have a transformed life – like the larva which one day will fly as a butterfly.

Outside in nature there are swarms of butterflies. Some are as big as a hand with wings in deep blue shades. Some are yellow or red, others brownish with beige spots. They are magnificent creatures! Many of those who ask for counseling at the centre are like those butterflies, though often injured. Subjected to a hard and brutal reality they are not able to "lift their wings" again.

Most of my contact is with adults – people from church and parents of the disabled children. They speak about their pain, then we pray and try to find a clearing in the dark together. It is really not easy to find some kind of meaning in the incomprehensible. These days are demanding days that do something to me. Everyone who wants to talk to me carries with them a major trauma. They have brutal experiences with violence, poverty and abuse, and their sorrow is great. Most of them have never before dared to share their painful experiences with others.

Being their conversation partner is a great responsibility. I often feel like I fall short. I am very humbled in the face of the will to live and the great courage these individuals display – and their simple, yet strong faith – in the midst of the worst possible circumstances. Many of them simply look at me and say: "We know that you will understand, *Doctora*."

What is it they see? My own disability? Or something of the love God has given me for them?

A mother comes to me with her sorrow and guilt. Her boy has cerebral palsy, a disease resulting from brain damage. The control centre for movement is not working properly, so the boy has many involuntary movements. He is furthermore unable to talk with words, only with sounds. Since he is unable to walk, he is sitting in a wheelchair.

The mother is telling me that when the boy was born his skin was completely yellow. But it was the rainy season, so he could not be out in the sun to "bleach" the jaundice. He was supposed to be treated with phototherapy at the hospital, but it cost five dollars (roughly 3 pounds), and the family couldn't afford it. The end result was that the boy suffered brain damage and received a huge and permanent disability – because no one would give him a treatment that cost five dollars!

Another one comes to the centre and tells me with a quiver about his trauma from the earthquake. After he and his brother had dined together, they were walking down the street while talking. Suddenly the earth began trembling. A wall caves in and falls over this man's brother, the next moment his brother disappears. He is all of a sudden surrounded by an unfamiliar landscape. All the houses have collapsed, and no signs or streets tell him where he is. He is left completely disoriented. Worse yet are all the screams he hears from people who are trapped under the rubble. At first the cries are heard clearly, then a little weaker, until after a few days they fade into silence.

"That is the worst," he says to me, "having survived, but being unable to do anything to help!"

A woman recounts when she and her elderly father are held captive. They were in separate rooms, but it was easy to understand what was happening next door. Her father was tortured, while she was systematically raped. This woman heard her father scream. Finally shots were fired, and everything went silent. Without later being able to explain how it happened, she was able to escape. She fled to another part of the country. She then realized that she was pregnant and gave birth to a severely disabled child. Now she is constantly fearful and struggling with many unanswered questions.

I have no answers. Why all these evil and bad things happen I don't know. I can only be present in the pain and walk part of the way alongside each of these seriously injured "butterflies" that I encounter. What I can do is to show them that they have value. I can listen to what they have to say. That they will get the hours and days they need. That there will be no condemnation of all the choices they have made. That I care about those who come to me to talk. That God cares about them! That I can believe for them when they have little faith themselves – believe that they some day in the future will find a better life.

Lord!

Let the cries inside of me

be filtered through your love

- so that one day they will be transformed into praise!

Lord!

Let the pain inside of me

be enveloped by your nacre,

in the deep,

where you see.

Carry me through the night,

you who are the Morning Star.

Amen.

15

To live

I live at the centre during the first period in Colombia. It is a strange experience, because right outside heavy traffic speeds past, day and night – trailers on the way over the mountains with valuable cargo of food and other goods. The house shakes and so do I.

Then I move to the countryside. I have been able to rent part of a house, and move in here together with my new assistant, Colombian Laura. We are well protected by four Rottweilers. If someone who doesn't belong to the household comes too close, these dogs are not to be trifled with.

Laura is full and round and dances while walking. Her zest for life is great! Together we sit on the terrace in the early evenings and enjoy the song of cicadas, while fireflies glimmer like tiny lanterns between the branches of the large avocado tree.

The house owner is an elderly gentleman called Laurencio. He enjoys spending time with Laura and me. In the afternoons he comes to keep us company, and tells us many great stories from his interesting years as a Colombian national politician. He has now become a widower, his children are all busy, and life is therefore at times quite lonely for Laurencio.

Our host is a lover of animals. His horse roams freely in the garden and serves as a lawnmower. Laurencio also has a very angry, but talkative parrot with long red and green feathers. He sits tethered to a stick between two roof pillars. There he mutters angrily while moving back and forth on the stick. Only when Laurencio approaches with a small treat does a good-natured sound come from the bird.

At night we have to use mosquito nets. Nevertheless I keep getting bitten by small, almost invisible mosquitoes. Every night Laura needs to rub lemon slices on my badly stung legs. The lemon juice helps against the itch and prevents the bites from becoming infected.

When it rains, my bed also becomes wet. One night I even wake up with a cockroach on my nose. But I take it with great calm. After all a missionary must put up with some things.

However, one night I begin to suspect trouble. Something is moving underneath my shoulders! The next morning the mattress is investigated, but – no, nothing can be found. It continues like this for weeks. In the end I have to be strict and demand that the mattress is removed. That is when we realize what has bothered me. A small mouse is standing on two legs and glancing up with sparkling black pearl eyes. Mother mouse has created a nice nest for her many unruly kids in my mattress. Underneath the bed she has a food store of flies, butterflies and other delicious dishes.

It is while I live here at the house of Laurencio that God starts showing me the need for processing some of my own inner wounds. When faced with the great suffering of others I feel completely lost. Many times I encounter deep unresolved pain that I myself carry. Something must be done here!

Who can help me with this? I have heard of something called Ellel Ministries. They are located in England. This is how I again pack my suitcase to cross the Atlantic. This time I travel in the opposite direction to attend school. NETS 12 is an Ellel course that I will be a part of for the next five months. The course will transform me completely. I will never be the same again.

16

Pierrepont

Ellel Ministries is a Christian, non-denominational missions organization. Their vision is to welcome people, teach them about the kingdom of God and be a tool for healing to those who need it. Ellel is represented in many countries. The international training centre for the organization, Ellel Pierrepont, lies in Surrey outside of London.

This was the place I found my way to on a cold April day in 2003. And what a reception they gave me! A wheelchair ramp had been built so that I could enter the main building without trouble, and a well adjusted single room had been prepared for me. My personal assistant was accommodated in the neighbouring room.

I thrived in Surrey! From all my years as a student, I was no stranger to long days of teaching and practical training, so that was okay. For me Pierrepont also became a spiritual home, a place where I could meet like-minded believers.

The centre is beautifully situated with wild life and magnificent grounds as part of the property. The river that passes by here is flanked by old gardens, and the riverside is a popular spot for silence and reflection. I had my electric wheelchair as transportation and used to race it around the area.

One afternoon I did not show up to our lectures. They reported me missing. After some hours the odd-job man of the centre found me where I was entirely stuck with all four wheels in the sandy riverbank. I was sorry to have missed valuable lecture time, and regretted creating so much trouble – yet I rejoiced over the opportunity to venture out into nature on my own!

After getting stuck that one time my wheelchair often got called *Pierrepont's black sheep.* The chair's reputation didn't exactly improve when on an outing far away one of the wheels punctured. Once again it was a full emergency and kind souls helped me and the chair home on the centre's truck.

Never was a bad word uttered because of this. Great understanding was always shown for my need to get out and enjoy nature, without having a "nanny" in tow. Even when the wheelchair tore up carpet tiles in the lecture hall, they were just glued back in place with a smile! Yes, I was really welcomed and well taken care of in every way.

Much of the teaching and intercession at the Ellel centre was felt deeply. Part of what was happening here was familiar to me as a psychiatrist. At the same time this experience at Pierrepont was different, because God was consulted all the time. And the answers from Him who created us and gave us life were very specific.

We started each day with worship. One such morning, midway through the worship, God came to me in a powerful picture: I saw myself sitting on His lap, just as I used to sit on Daddy's lap as a little girl and was fed shaved apple. To "cut abbles", as my dad would call it in his charming southern accent, was the best thing I knew! So when God gave me this picture, I intuitively thought of something good. Great was my alarm therefore when he asked me:

"Beate, are you willing to walk with me through the valley of weeping and painful cries?"

Oh dear! I did not much want to do it, but I answered yes. Then I was filled with a deep peace.

That was that. Nothing else happened that day in connection with it.

The next morning I woke up after a dream. In the dream I had been standing by a large pool of dark water that was impossible to see through. Beside me stood Jesus.

"This is your life's unshed tears," He said.

The pool was huge and deep.

The next two days the teaching at Pierrepont was about being accepted, in contrast to being rejected or abandoned. I sat at the back of the classroom and sobbed through two full long days. Over and over God gave me pictures; they passed in review as on an inner invisible film canvas. I saw all of it – the times at the hospital both as a child and as an adult, the loneliness, the despair, the disappointment, and all the letdowns – everything came before me. One face after another appeared before me of those I had met. So I sat and cried and cried. I used up two boxes of paper handkerchiefs alone.

The strange thing was that no one came running to comfort me. They obviously realized that it would not have helped. No one was to come between me and God. No empty words like, "hush, hush, it will be all right!" would cover up the pain which in reality was too great to embrace.

But God was there. He was present in my great sorrow over everything that had been shattered. For so many years I had swallowed down this pain, before I now made room for it and it was brought up to the surface. It was in truth a walk through the vale of tears, an experience I will never forget!

After these two days I woke up the next morning after another clear dream. This time I saw myself sitting at the edge of the pool I had seen in the first dream. I sat there kicking my feet, with Jesus beside me. But the pool was now completely empty! The only water to be seen was two small puddles at the bottom of the pool. This water was also completely transparent and reflected the blue sky!

When I speak to others about my dreams I am often met with head-shaking doubt. In England, however, I meet people who in their own encounters with God have had experiences like mine. One day I told the director of the centre Jill Southern-Jones about the dreams and visions I had experienced. She looked straight at me with searching eyes and said:

"Beatriz, when God gives someone a vision, He usually wants this person to be part of the fulfilment of the vision."

Those were big words for a little lady in a wheelchair.

Slowly but surely it dawned on me that God does not need mediators to convey his message to an individual. The Bible is full of stories of how God spoke to ordinary people: Joseph, Abraham, Moses, Samuel, David, Gideon, Mary, Paul and Peter are only a few of the many who had the privilege of hearing God speak directly to them. For us who read the story of their lives, they are special heroes of faith. However, many of them were weak and had character flaws, and some had physical deficiencies. They, like us, had a lot to struggle with in their lifetime! Furthermore they could not read the Bible and understand that the difficulties they lived through would end. There was no blueprint for their life. But when it was important for them to step into God's plan, He spoke directly to them. Since God then is the same today, why would He not speak directly to individuals now? Meanwhile we are also so fortunate to have the Bible, and can test the truth in what we possibly see and hear in dreams and visions against it. We know that God can never contradict Himself. He will never ask us to do something that contradicts what the Bible says about what is right and wrong.

In previous times God often chose weak people to do impossible things. Thus there would never be any doubt about who should receive the credit for what happened. I had myself landed in an impossible situation, but at Pierrepont I understood little by little: I walk together with a God for whom all things are possible!

17

Peñas Blancas

After the time in England my path travels to Norway for a short while. I am about to sell my apartment in Oslo and have my earthly goods moved to Colombia. A lot of it is given away, but the electric armchair needs to be part of the load to be moved. Furthermore Christmas decorations, crockery and old notes are packed into all sorts of boxes. My dad's old paintings also come along. It is quite a bit of a hassle!

The evening I am back in Colombia, I am coming to my new home. It is a small brick house near the village of Peñas Blancas (white cliffs). The village is named after the white sandstone cliffs high in the mountains on the opposite side of the Quindio River. Chief Calarcá, the legendary *cacique*, is supposed to be buried here. Together with his men and a large treasure of gold, he allegedly sought refuge in the mountain caves here. Many of those who in recent times have sought the legendary gold treasure have found their way into the caves, but several of them then never returned.

The first one to greet me is the kitten Saturnino. He is white and black and has ruffled fur. Saturnino actually belongs to the neighbour, but he has caused a small accident in a bed there and has been thrown outside. Now the kitten has taken refuge in the newly built, almost empty house that will be mine. He snuggles up to my wheelchair and when a willing soul lifts him up to me, he purrs with loud excitement. Without any further difficulties

Saturnino curls up on my chest and falls asleep. He too has found a new home.

Soon there will be more family members. Since I live in the countryside a good distance from the main road, it is wise to keep a dog. And one day in April, the puppy Lucas and I are presented to each other. It happens when I am visiting the small mountain town of Salento, which is secluded between deep valleys and high mountains. Coming here is like stepping into another century. In Salento proud riders sit high on horseback and ride through the streets. The rider has a *poncho* across his shoulders, a *machete* knife in his belt, and on his head he wears a wide-brimmed straw hat. Overlooking the narrow streets hang colourful wooden balconies, and the old wooden houses seem protected from the new century's demands for change. At the marketplace fruit and sweets are sold from stalls, while the fragile, vibrating notes of the Andes flutes sound across the square. Small restaurants offer pork rind, various soups and tasty trout in garlic sauce. The fish is served on a plate of *patacon*, flakes of rolled out banana fried in oil. As time has passed and tourists have discovered Salento, many small handicraft businesses have emerged. Riding tours are arranged alongside the beautiful, lush valley.

When the tropical night turns the day off in Salento, the wrought iron lanterns give a weak glimmer to orient oneself afterwards. From snowy mountains rising high up towards the sky melting water flows in torrents, and in the valley below the village the Quindío river rustles its eternal song. At the early dawn large flocks of herons fly along the river and in through the Cocora valley. The white wings are coloured golden pink in the first sunbeams of the day.

This is where Lucas was born. By all accounts he is a French poodle, but Lucas probably has a more doubtful pedigree. He is two days old when he is lifted up on my lap and starts licking my cheek. From my side it is love at first sight. The puppy has not yet opened his eyes, so he cannot see me, but he too chooses me. I will be his new *mamá* and after two months he finds his place as a new family member at Peñas Blancas.

The kitten Saturnino takes his role as adoptive father for Lucas, the puppy, most seriously. To date, ten years later, Lucas still behaves like a cat: every morning the dog licks his paw and uses it to wash his face, just like cats do! Lucas and Saturnino are inseparable friends. They are boisterous in their play and come up with countless pranks.

At Easter I bring branches in from the orange tree in the garden. I hang hand-painted Easter eggs on them, some of which have found their long way across the Atlantic. One morning when I come out into the living room, an unexpected sight greets me: the floor is covered with eggshells! And on top of the dining table Saturnino is sitting with his paw between the orange branches. He has been caught. He is the one who has been pushing down all the decorated Easter eggs. Underneath the table Lucas is sitting with an expectant look in his eyes. The dog has a painted wooden egg in his mouth.

When the two rascals spot me, they dash like greased lightning out to the basket they share. There they stay put and cling to each other while awaiting their punishment. They know full well that they have done something they shouldn't have, but the temptation during the quiet morning hours was too great. It is sad that the eggs that survived four months at sea, had to give in to two of Peñas Blancas' small four-footed *casiques*, the uncrowned chiefs of the house. They are of course not given any punishment.

Saturnino is very curious. He loves to climb up into the large avocado tree in the garden, where he makes noises that sound confusingly like birds chirping. Finally, we have to place a collar with a bell on him so too many colourful small birds will not end up as dinner for kitty.

The two four-legged creatures hold indoor sprinting competitions every evening. Then they rush from one end of the house to the other – back and forth. They never get bored! The only thing that can stop them is if one of the big spiders enters. Then Lucas and Saturnino come to a sudden stop, and it is time to use poison spray and broomsticks as weapons. Since I live in the middle of a plantation area, I am relatively often visited by snakes and spiders. One time I am bitten by such a spider and have to endure a long week with a swollen arm, fever and headache – just because a microscopic yellow-white insect came a little too close. Yes, there are some experiences that are completely new for a north-Norwegian small whale that has ended up in the Andes.

But mostly everything goes well. I thrive among climbing plants, bird chirping and tropical sunsets. Sometimes the heat is an ordeal, but little by little it has become okay for me. The dengue mosquitoes are continually a nuisance however. One of their bites causes creeping and sharp febrile contractions, headaches and physical exhaustion.

Once a week I have pastoral care at my office. Then I first have to go to Armenia and pick up my co-intercessor and the person who is seeking help. There are in fact no buses where I live and very few have their own car. It is also dangerous to walk along the highways alone; security is no joke in Colombia. In this area the police are very aware of what foreigners may undergo. That someone breaks into your house or car, or attempts to do so, is not a pleasant experience. The same applies to sabotage or kidnapping attempts. Sometimes threats come a bit too close for comfort, and then it may happen that I am asked to leave the country quickly.

But mighty angels keep watch! I sleep well and am not afraid. Since I teach in a lot of different churches in Armenia, it can mean many late nights and we then pray for angels' protection. If it is ever necessary for our invisible guardians to become visible to those who wish to harm us, we trust that this will happen too.

"Now, Lord, consider their threats and enable your servants to speak your word with great boldness. Stretch out your hand to heal and perform signs and wonders through the name of your holy servant Jesus."[6]

One time when I come home after having travelled, there is something that is simply not right. Saturnino is ill! I find him where he is hiding behind the washing machine. The cat cannot walk, and he is complaining and groaning. Lucas is furious at everyone else and defends his cat-friend as best he can.

It turns out that Saturnino has had a brain haemorrhage. He furthermore has a severe blood clot in one leg. My sorrow is great over what has happened!

We do what we can to help Saturnino, but the little cat suffers severely. One morning a few days later, I wake up with tears running down my cheeks. I have had a very clear dream again, and this time I have seen Saturnino asleep on Jesus' lap. His nail-scarred hands slowly stroke the back of the cat. Then Saturnino wakes up, and in the dream he jumps with joy down on to the ground and walks on with his tail held high.

I realize what the dream means. In the heat of the day, I say farewell to Saturnino. I choose to stay with him as his little life ebbs away. The next day I lay Saturnino to rest in a small grave under a blue guayacán.

---

6 Acts 4, 29-30

18

Decision

It is August and the guayacáns are blooming. Along the roads and streets they stand like great giants with golden crowns in yellow, pink or blue. The wind causes the small lily-shaped flowers to shake and sends them like colourful rain to the ground. There the flowers remain like an outstretched soft blanket.

I am on my way to the airport to meet some guests. Seven people, who will lead our first international Ellel Conference here in Colombia, are arriving. I and others from the local Ellel group have travelled around for months to present this project to church leaders in the counties around Armenia. I am a little bit overtired, especially because I have come down with dengue fever. I am seriously considering whether this work is something I can continue doing or whether my time in Colombia is perhaps coming to an end. I am after all on disability pension and do not have much strength to exert.

On my way to the airport I stop at the petrol station to fill the tank in the car. A little boy comes up to me. He cannot be more than four years old. The boy is a hawker, obviously one of many children who need to help provide for their families. His clothes are filthy, and his face and hands are dirty, but when he looks up at me, he greets me with a big smile.

"Thall de ladee puy peeouuth?" In his strange, childish language it must mean "Shall the lady buy peanuts?"

I see that he has an untreated cleft lip. Now he holds a small fist up expectantly. In it he holds a cornet full of peanuts. All the time he stares at me, the lady in the nice car.

In a powerful flash of light I suddenly observe that we are not alone. Jesus stands behind the little peanut salesman! His hands are resting on the boy's small shoulders. The Lord looks seriously at me and quietly says:

"You can go, Beate, but I will stay!"

Of course I buy peanuts, and the boy runs happily and satisfied away, probably to buy an *arepa*, a flat little corn bread, and a glass of milk. Perhaps this is the only food and drink he will have today.

God has spoken, just like He has spoken before. Momentarily I know without a shadow of a doubt that my place is here, at the foot of the high Colombian mountains. Where Jesus is, I also want to be.

Afterwards we experience wonderful conference days with valuable teaching. Topics covered include trauma and despair, being able to forgive, and much, much more. We also enjoy a visit to the butterfly gardens and the beautiful Coffee Park. When we have international visitors, we usually take them to see the magnificent botanical gardens where butterflies fly around and to the largest amusement park in South America.

At the conclusion of the conference I am asked to become the official representative for Ellel in Colombia. A little shakily I accept the challenge.

Later that year I get to teach about forgiveness myself. It happens in a church in a town to the north of Armenia. Together with my personal assistant Griselda and a small Colombian Ellel team I hold a small conference in the city. I speak of some of my own experiences with forgiveness. The audience hear about how God met me when my own tears were frozen to ice. Then Jesus came and said He wanted to spell the word *forgiveness* to me. I could see a blood coloured flower in His heart. A root then starts to grow from the flower over to my own heart, and a flower just like the one in Jesus' heart shoots up there. I understand that it is the flower of forgiveness.

By myself I cannot forgive. Even though I know that I must forgive to receive forgiveness, it is humanly impossible to forgive those who have crushed me and robbed me of everything that used to be my life. Yes, I may even have accused God for the things that have happened. So if I ever should be able to forgive, it is only Jesus who can help me do it. But I must choose to allow Him in. I need to allow Jesus to guide me through the jungle of pain and bitterness.

I look out upon the crowd at the conference. On the front row I notice a man and a woman – two hardened faces that slowly dissolve into tears. I can see how their lips move as they repeat the personalized prayer for forgiveness, slowly read aloud by me, and I see how something sets them free. Something has been released, and they can let hatred and hopelessness go. They can give everything to Jesus!

After I finish teaching, they both come forward for prayer. It turns out that the woman has been physically abused by her husband, and has developed paralysis in one of her legs. Now she has to use leg braces to walk. The man who comes to the front has a disfigured face. This has happened at his job as he fell into a tank of strong acid. So he has been injured for life, but without getting any kind of compensation for it. On the contrary, he has lost his job because of his long sick leave. His wife leaves him next. So he is left on his own, lonely and with a bitter heart. Here at this meeting something critical has happened for both the man and the woman in front of me. With the help of Jesus they have been able to forgive. I can see a new hope shining in both their faces. A huge burden has been lifted off them, and they can now move forward again.

These stories are only two of many that have been shared over the years as testimonies of what Jesus has done in people's lives. I continually understand more clearly why it is important not to give up, but to stay where God has placed me. I myself am weak and small, but it is not important as long as Jesus can use me to reach out to others with who He is and what He can do. He is more than strong enough in my weakness.

19

The testimony of mosquitoes and cold floor tiles

I wake up because I am freezing. I see Lucas lying at the end of my bed. He has borrowed a good piece of the Norwegian duvet I have brought here. He now lies there snoring with small grunts. Only a small portion of his nose is sticking out from underneath the sleeping bag he has made of the corner of the duvet. I personally love the early dawn before the heat has been let loose in Peñas Blancas. Here in the heights nights are cold, often as low as zero degrees.

This morning Lucas' new baby brother, a cat called Pixi, has opened the insect screen on the window to crawl out for a morning stroll. A cool breeze makes the thin cotton curtains flutter softly. A large flock of small, green parrots chatter away as they fly above the house. They sit down on the roof of my neighbour's house and in the trees around my house. Their happy prattle wakes me up with a smile. My gaze falls on the bird feeder, where two blue birds are enjoying the last vestige of yesterday's banana. Two hummingbirds with the blue-green shade of phosphorus are fighting for space at the sugar water container. Their wings flap like invisible fans as the tiny birds are standing still in the air underneath the patio roof. The sun slowly comes up over the high mountains to the east. Fingers of light stretch down towards the valley floor and drive the sheets of morning fog away. A new day is about to begin. Thank you,

God, that I am alive! Today is Sunday, and at church await hours full of worship, teaching and ministry.

Pastor André is very inspired during the preaching today. He stretches his hands towards the congregation and prays for healing for everyone with neurological damage. It is a very hot day, and I can feel how sweat is running down my back. It is as if I am burning where I am sitting in the wheelchair.

After the service I spend time in conversation with different people. I am only ready to go back home again after several hours.

Then I notice that the mosquitoes are agitated and bite my feet. Strange! I have never felt this before, have I? Earlier I only felt the itch, not the actual bites.

Many years have passed since the September day when I woke up paralyzed. Many are those who have been praying for me, and God has listened. I have gradually regained more of my physical mobility. My life is no longer limited to lying on my back in a hospital bed! I can almost use my hands normally again, and with high crutches I am also able to walk a few steps. My legs unfortunately still feel icy cold, because my blood circulation is lousy. The skin is without normal sensation. When Griselda massages my legs, I still feel a deep, burning pain. Massage is however necessary to counteract the considerable swellings I tend to get in the tropical heat.

Such treatment is also needed this Sunday. When we come home, Griselda and I first eat a long overdue dinner. I then sit down in the reclining chair with my legs high, and Griselda starts to massage them.

Then I suddenly roar. I begin to sob uncontrollably. *I can feel her touching me without it hurting!* I have recovered normal sensation in both legs again!

Some moments pass before I can pull myself together enough to tell Griselda that a miracle has happened. A miracle! Of course that was the reason I could feel the mosquitoes bite! Thank you, good God, for the mosquitoes and their eager testimony!

The next day I sit in the shower a long, long time and enjoy the miracle – that I can feel the wet, cold floor tiles underfoot and the cool water trickling down my legs. Tears of gratitude are flowing down over this magnificent miracle that has happened in the middle of everyday life. Yet again my Lord has intervened!

So the burning sensation I felt along my spine during the prayer of the pastor was no ordinary heat. It was the Holy Spirit who touched me and repaired the massive neurological damage from so many years ago. It happened quietly in the back of the church. No one laid their hands on me, but God was there!

Every morning to this date, I will rejoice over the sensation of the fresh, running water and the cool floor tiles underneath my feet. I never get tired of this feeling that I thought was lost forever.

20

The sting of death

A damp, oppressive heat fills the day. The rays of the sun are not able to penetrate the thick, hazy air. From the north heavy blue-black clouds come drifting in. At noon it is almost dark. I sit on the bench underneath the canopy of my patio. The cat and dog are both anxious and press themselves tightly to both sides of me. This is how they usually react when there is high seismic activity, so I ask myself if another earthquake is coming. But no, everything is quiet. Nevertheless, the feeling of eeriness does not leave me.

In the evening I am going to a service at church. We have a good distance to drive into Armenia, so my assistant and I start the trip pretty early. Already at the roundabout east of the city we encounter police barriers. Something has happened! A large area is blocked off, but the police will not of course tell us the reason for it. We have to take long detours to reach the church.

When we get there all the lights are out. But were we not supposed to have a service? Have I been mistaken about the day?

We discover a stooped figure coming towards us. It is a man. With tears in his eyes he tells us that two of the brothers in the church have been killed – gunned down in broad daylight! They were on their daily jog around the block when the *sicario* came on a fast motorcycle. The hired assassin shot and killed Alfonso. Then his brother Alvaro got so upset that he ran after the gunman. Thus he was also shot.

The following Sunday the church is packed with grieving individuals. We all sit there, so helpless. Two chairs right in front of me are empty. Those were the seats of Alfonso and Alvaro. Both brothers were faithful churchgoers. I am unable to stop the flow of tears. The widows, the bereaved children and siblings of Alfonso and Alvaro – they are all there. I feel a deep sorrow. So does God, I sense. The Lord Himself mourns all the lost lives in this country where a human life seems to hold so little value. I pray for those who have lost not one, but two of their own.

When the service is over and everyone marches out, I spot the old lady. It is the mother of the two who are no longer here. She comes down the aisle slowly. She glances at me where I am sitting in my wheelchair at the back of the church. Then she throws herself into my arms. I hold her tightly as tears flow down. I refrain from saying anything, but am just present with her.

A month passes by. Then Elvira calls. She tells me that Paco did not return home last night. Paco had previously worked together with Alfonso and Alvaro. The days pass without Paco turning up. We begin to sense danger. A bone-chilling certainty that something is very wrong takes hold. After a week they find him shot, with terrible injuries.

Also this Sunday the church is filled to bursting. Now another chair is standing empty. Paco was a worshipper at the church, and like Alfonso and Alvaro he had his regular seat right in front of me. His face used to beam when he raised his hands to praise his Lord and God. Now he stands before the heavenly altar where pain does not exist and death takes no life.

Paco's ten year old son Juan has also come to church. His eyes are dry. Tears seem to have frozen to ice in this little boy who now has to help provide for his mother, grandmother and sister. Suddenly Juan is standing right in front of me. His eyes are empty. It is as if he is gazing into a great nothingness.

"Can I give you a hug?" I ask.

He nods slightly and moves closer to me. Carefully I put my arms around the slender body of the boy. He is completely silent at first, but then he begins to sob. He bellows out his great pain, tears flow, and his body is shaking. No one at church makes any disturbing comments; they understand that Juan needs to be left alone in his grief. And such great sorrow! So much pain! So much injustice!

I am not letting go of Juan. After an hour his tears subside, and the little boy is no longer a child. I notice the determined expression in his little face. He seems to have found strength to move ahead. I personally know that it was not my arms, but the arms of Jesus, which held Juan.

When we exit the church, the beautiful summer's day is about to become cloudy. Large dark clouds are drifting in from the north, and the first raindrops fall to the ground. God weeps in the rain.

21

A sacrifice

Part of the problem with having a chronic disease or disability is that you are never fully treated. Complicating factors often appear along the way.

One day I start having lower back pain. It is like strong sciatica. As time passes it gets increasingly worse. Finally, I am unable to lie in bed at night, and must sleep sitting up in the recliner. X-rays are being taken of my back, and the pictures are sent to a specialist in Norway. It turns out that the hip prosthesis has come loose and has made a hole in the bone tissue it was attached to. The pain is excruciating. Fifteen months will pass before I receive any help with it. Until then I have many long and painful vigils. In the daytime I still manage to continue with counselling and teaching, but I am getting dangerously tired. The more tired I am, the harder it is to have good boundaries in my work. Car rides especially become a nightmare for me with all the bumpy roads here.

Eventually I get to go to Norway. The hip replacement surgery goes well, and little by little I recover again. I am also offered a prosthesis in the hip that was so severely injured many years ago. The same medical possibilities were not available at that time as they are today. Yes, the surgeon believes that I will walk again! After fourteen years in a wheelchair, it is no wonder that my joy and expectation is great.

The following year I am ready for the planned procedure. Unfortunately, serious complications arise during anaesthesia. Too much time passes without sufficient oxygen. So I end up in a respirator. My throat is now so swollen that I struggle to breathe. For this reason I have to sit and sleep for several weeks after coming out of the respirator. Lack of oxygen during surgery has also given me trouble with my short-term memory. Fortunately, my joy of reading helps me. Only six weeks later I return to Colombia. During the first few months after the surgery I devour a number of books in Norwegian, English and Spanish, and little by little my memory returns.

The hip surgery itself was successful, so I can now walk again. It is amazing! I surely must use crutches, but my legs are now of equal length. This enables me – without pain, and with great eagerness – to set off every single day. I thoroughly enjoy the opportunity to use the outdoor pool at the housing estate where I live in Colombia.

But then I start hurting again. This time the pain is like a ring around my right thigh. Little by little it is so severe that I can neither walk nor lie down. I have to find the wheelchair again. With it we often make small trips around the neighbourhood where I live. In front comes Pixi, the cat, with his tail held high. Then I follow in the wheelchair, with Lucas, the dog, on a leash. My assistant Griselda walks at the back as "the engine" of our small procession. One of the neighbours asks if I have become too lazy to walk. The question cuts me deep down in my heart.

At my next check-up with the surgeon in Norway we find the reason for the recent pain. The prosthesis has slipped out through the femur and the bone has broken in two. It looks terrible on x-rays and must be treated as quickly as possible.

The surgeon and I have a long conversation about this. The road ahead of me is no joke, especially since great risk is associated with giving me anaesthesia. Bluntly the surgeon tells me that if I would choose to stay in Norway, he could have offered me a reconstruction of the whole hip. It would have required several years of treatment including bone tissue transplanted to the hip. But since I am returning to Colombia, he needs to remove the prosthesis yet again. This time the damage is so great that nothing further can be done. No new surgery can be offered, and I will thus be unable to walk again.

I make it through the surgery. At the worst moment I have another divine encounter. I see Jesus at the end of the operating table. He asks me if I am willing to go through this for Him.

I understand what He means. If I do not go through this operation, pain will make it impossible for me to return to Colombia. Just the travel there takes almost twenty six hours, with all the toll this takes on my body. But I remember what happened many years ago, when a little boy asked me to buy peanuts, and I made a decision to stay in Colombia. So, quo vadis? Where are you going, Lord? Jesus will return to Colombia, and also this time, I will follow Him there!

One morning after my return to Colombia, Jesus wakes me up with a question that is a bit strange:

"Beate, what happens to biological tissue that is removed from the human body during surgery?"

I know the answer. The tissue is burned.

"In this way your hip was a burnt offering to me," says the Lord.

It takes a few moments before I fully understand what He means. I know what a burnt offering is, but this is different. In order to continue my ministry for Jesus in Colombia, I had to give up the opportunity for further surgery – and with it, the possibility of walking again. The tissue that was removed from my body during the recent hip surgery was burnt. God clearly knew what this means to me. He now confirms that He knew this and that He considers it a sacrifice to Him. My pain has not been in vain. Right there I am filled with a deep peace. Once again the Lord has provided meaning in the midst of the meaningless.

22

The race of my life

Life does not become easier than before, but little by little I regain some of my mobility. Eventually I manage to get out of bed by myself, and I learn how to lift the limp leg with the help of the other leg. I just regain my balance too. However, in the midst of this I carry a silent sorrow of once again having lost hope that I will be able to walk again.

Before it gets better, it will be much worse.

During the three months that have passed since I returned to Colombia, I have felt ever more feeble and unwell. It makes me quite depressed. I often have headaches, and my shoulders and legs have started aching. I also sense an increasing pressure in my chest. My hip that had the latest operation soon swells up and turns violet.

When I finally get to the doctor it is almost too late. My blood pressure has become so low that it cannot be measured. It is noticeable for I am very dizzy. It turns out that I have carried an infection since the operation, but it is only by giving me blood poisoning (sepsis) that it has made itself known. I am now thoroughly medicated and treated according to the rules of the medical art.

The fever is high, and I hallucinate. I am sure that I hear the songs of angels, and I am convinced that I will die. One night I ask loudly into the silence of the room where the beautiful song surrounds me: "Will I come to heaven now?"

The answer is clear, with the same voice I know so well after all the times I have heard it over the years, "No, Beate, not yet."

I am so, so tired! But I survive! By the skin of my teeth I get through this too.

In the midst of this I watch a video clip about the athlete Derek who was injured during the Olympic Games in Barcelona in 1992. I also read Ken Symington's book *Loved as never before*, where the same story is mentioned.

Athletic star Derek was the favourite and ran for gold. But four hundred metres before the finish he heard a pop and fell down with agonizing pain in one thigh. The hamstring of one of the largest thigh muscles had snapped. Despite the excruciating pain he got back on his feet and hobbled on.

Nobody knows for sure how the next thing happened, but all of a sudden a slightly older man runs out on the track. He has ploughed his way through masses of people and security guards along the way – out to the injured man. This man was the runner's father!

"You don't have to finish the race," his father says.

"Yes, I must," the son replies.

"Then let's finish it together, my boy!" his dad resolves.

Oh, how I recognize myself in that story! I also have severe pain in the thigh, just as I also have this determination not to give up the race of my life! With weeping I haul myself forward, while all the time leaning heavily on my heavenly Father. He is stroking my hair while patting me reassuringly on my cheek.

"It will all go well," He says. "You are so clever! I am proud of you! And, I am here, with you."

In truth it is the Lord who carries me. I fall asleep in the reassurance that I am not alone on the last stretch to the finish line. My father carries me when I am too tired to walk myself. He has certainly not given up.

I can choose for myself. If I want to, I can give up now. But for me that is no real option. Together with the Lord I would much rather continue. It doesn't move fast, but together we move forward, step by step, though ever so slowly.

It is early evening. Where I lie in the recliner, the full moon is shining on me. Outside I see the flowering flame tulip tree with its mighty crown of fiery red flowers. I am in Colombia! Along with Jesus! This is where I belong!

23

In green pastures beside still waters

It is a great privilege when people open their heart up to you and allow you to share in their pain and struggle. In this room of trust where door after door is opened cautiously, Jesus can enter in. Pastoral care is essentially about this: being available for Jesus so that He can cleanse, heal, and glue back together the pieces of a life that has been broken.

When I did my specialist training in psychiatry, my supervising physician would take one vacation every year by himself. He was married, had two children and was happy together with them, but once a year he nonetheless ventured on a long fishing trip all by himself. This really surprised me – until I understood from my own experience that it is necessary to retreat from time to time, to be unavailable, and to be free from demands to offer anything at all.

Few things can compare to helping people at the most personal level. At the same time it is one of the most demanding tasks there is, because you make use of every part of yourself. If you do not allow yourself a breather periodically, you may find yourself exhausted from the battle or burned out.

I personally try to obey the biblical commandment to keep the Sabbath holy. I think the commandment has been given to us humans for our own good! We are not machines or robots, so we need rest to recharge our batteries and to find new motivation. We need time to be creative, enjoy nature, maybe read a good book – and a book that is not related to our professional work or study. And what is most important: we need quality time with Jesus.

Here in Colombia I have a "secret" resting place. The spot is placed between green "sugar top" mountains, in a deep valley beyond the ancient university city of Manizales. Here you find a large hotel complex with hot springs. It is a long drive there, taking just about three hours, but it is well worth it.

The path to the cottages runs through Colombia's coffee district. Here the fields and slopes are filled with lush, deep green coffee bushes. With their white starry flowers and the ripening red coffee beans side by side, they are a magnificent sight. In between lie great *fincas* with both small and large buildings. They have tiles of baked clay, and their red, yellow or green arches provide welcome shade. I glimpse window shutters in passing, also in happy colours. The rural farmhouses resemble big dolls houses with smiling windows that wave at us as we pass, each *finca* revealing its own silent history with well-kept secrets from a bygone time. Yes, even the car ride here makes me happy!

After reaching our destination we are settled into a small cottage. It has bold, bright colours and is covered with a double layer of roof tiles. In the small living room there is a fireplace. Beside the fireplace, fragrant firewood is piled up ready for use. It will certainly come in handy where we are, two thousand metres above sea level.

The place is sheltered by high mountains. Ancient ferns grow here, as large as houses, and the surroundings are embellished with lots of beautiful, colourful flowers, hedges and trees. Cows graze on the hillsides, and when evening is approaching, they moo as if to complain. Since the mountains receive abundant rain, nature here takes on a particularly fresh and colourful appearance. Melt water from the snowy mountain glaciers also contributes.

Where I lodge, three large pools have been made from the water of hot springs, and many of the cottages have their own little bubble bath outside. The water comes in large pipes from the volcano, El Ruiz. This giant is active at irregular intervals, and not too long ago it had another eruption. The sour smell also reached Armenia, and north of us in Manizales and its neighbouring city Pereira, the streets were covered in volcanic ash. Temperatures rose intensely and the ground repeatedly trembled, sometimes above seven on the Richter scale! Airports were closed in both Colombia and neighbouring countries because clouds of smoke, steam and ash made it impossible to fly. But when Ruiz, the giant, slumbers, it is good to be by the hot springs. I rarely have more than a few days in a row here, but those days are all filled with the Lord's smile – right from the dawn of the day. Then I am accompanied by the soft contours of bluish mountains through the morning mist, and if it is the right time of the year, I hear swallows sing as they build their nest on the roof of the cottage entrance. They chirp their happy message and offer me an air show in the crystal clear morning air. When I get out of bed and place my feet on the icy cold floor tiles, joyful chills run through me, and I am enveloped by the silence of the slow sunrise.

I look outside. Around the cottage grows a sea of flowers on a dark green background. Flowers come in all sizes and shades of blue, purple, white, red and yellow, one more golden than the other. One of my favourites is the Agapanthus lilies. They stand in long rows of blue and white, like ballerinas with small flower skirts.

After the beautiful morning even more pleasures await. Steaming hot spring water softens my tired muscles, and exquisite cuisine gives new strength to both body and soul. The beautiful nature, silence and time of prayer and Bible reading revive my inner being. This is uplifting in every way.

When I am about to pay the bill after one of my stays, I see that someone has made a notation in the rubric for *User code*. Only one little word is written there: *Dios*. User code: God! Yes, with King David I can say of God: *"He makes me lie down in green pastures; he leads me beside still waters."* These still waters in bright green meadows are truly a gift from God to me in between ever busier days. I am sure that it is the Lord himself who gives me these days, and that He rejoices with me over all the small pleasures that make life so great. Rested and happy I return to the many challenges of daily life.

24

To paint with words and colours

Maria is an old acquaintance of mine. We have what may be called a therapeutic friendship.

For many years she has occasionally come to share her worry and frustration with me. Together we paint her life story with the help of words.

It is important for Maria that both the dog, Lucas, and the cat, Pixi, are present when she comes. She is particularly good friends with Pixi. She once had a cat that was like a child to her – a family member on four legs, a kitty who followed her as a shadow. Now her cat has disappeared.

Maria pulls her chair close to mine. She looks at me and then looks at me intently again, as if to find out if she can trust me enough to tell me what nobody else knows. She surely can. Over the years she has made many visits to me and there have been many conversations between us.

Maria has a great gift. She is a painter! She creates magnificent pictures in bright colours. She is particularly fond of painting with oil colours. Her canvasses are full of light and movement. She portrays lofty Calla lilies pressed against the ground by the wind of a dark night. She draws birds caught in wire traps. As only she is able to, she paints encaged freedom. Mountain formations in the distance perhaps resemble the sleeping body of a woman? Frothing ocean currents swirl past and wash everything away. In her world the bird's eye is red from repressed pain. A flaming sunset is lost behind the horizon, so will a new day then appear? Maria paints and paints.

Her last painting is named *Agapanthus in spring.* The erect lilies stand in the foreground with their mauve coloured small, bell-shaped flowers. There is an expectation in the picture.

What do these lilies wait for? What is the longing of Maria? The background is created by hurling ochre-yellow paint against the screen with great force. Anger and frustration tossed out with a strong and talented hand. The effect is a translucent landscape that draws one's thoughts towards dripping tears. Is it water that trickles down the canvas, like melt water from the distant snowy mountains, or are they frozen tears that have found their way into the light on the canvas? Maria paints and paints, with words and with brushes. And I get to take part.

25

To be in deep water

San Andrés Archipelago is Colombian and is located in the Caribbean Sea. With its swaying coconut palms and bright white beaches against the azure blue ocean, these coral reef islands are the very epitome of a tropical idyll. Here I have my second "secret" hiding place when weariness takes over and it's time for a small holiday.

Life here is lived at a slow tempo. Small fishing boats painted in bright colours are anchored in the bay and dip merrily up and down in the breeze. Now and then a sudden rain covers everything in its grey cloak. But most of the time the sun is shining from a high, cloudless sky. Then the seven blue shades of the ocean play like a piano rhapsody on the surface, until they are lost in the faintly green and yellow shades of sunlight as evening approaches. Underwater corals give a hint of grey-brown shadows on the surface. Light waves dance towards land where they gently ripple against the gunwale of numerous small boats at rest in the harbour. On the beaches, dark-skinned, buxom ladies in flowing, colourful dresses are wandering. They proudly lift their heads, as they each carry their large trays of coconut *bocados* or the other delicacies they sell.

The blazing tropical sunset is short and vibrant with colour as the sun quickly descends into the sea. At night I sleep with my windows open to fully enjoy the sea breeze. The waves thundering against the reef far out at sea become the cradle song that lulls me to sleep. During quiet nights they remind me of different coasts and sunsets a long, long time ago on the other side of the Atlantic.

I grew up as an islander, surrounded by the wild sea. Ever since I was a child I have had a natural inclination towards the sea. I already learned to dive ten years before I came to Colombia. Where I now live in the Andes Mountains, I am however far from breaking waves and deep blue sea. In the damp and quivering inland heat I often yearn for the coast and the cool sea breeze. So I find more or less good excuses and reasons for taking an occasional detour to the Caribbean Sea.

There I have over the years also been in deep water, literally speaking. For when the offer came to dive here at the San Andrés Islands, I was not slow to accept. Diving offers spectacular experiences of nature, and is an excellent way to enjoy the freedom of moving without any obstacles. The wheelchair stays on land, because in the water I am almost weightless. Deep down in the ocean I can lie still as the current moves me across exciting underwater landscapes.

Here in the azure blue depths of the tropical ocean I sense how God in heaven is watching everything and smiling upon the sun filled day of the planet. Our little, blue planet slowly rotates in the embrace of outer space. Two tiny humans slowly drift into the sea, while the sun playfully sparkles in the waves. God's mercy rests upon this fresh new morning. Deep down in the ocean, my diving buddy, Luis, and I are slowly gliding through the silent blue. Only bubbles dancing on the surface reveal our path in the depths. Hundreds of small silvery fish are shimmering around us as they join our expedition. A curious octopus peeks out from under the sand, before rushing off hurriedly. Up from behind red and blue coral reefs comes a troop of multicoloured peacock fish. A scorpion fish attempts to make itself invisible; with its jagged, mortal fins it is a reminder that life cannot be taken for granted. While busy catfish sweep the bottom of the sea with their yellow moustaches, a small puffer fish would like to play with the passing human guests. Huge sea fans sway as they dance, and massive sting rays glide in passing above us like huge birds in slow flight through the waters. The parrot fish is scraping small pieces of coral with its sharp beak. Shoals of both small and big fish are staring wide-eyed at us as we slowly float past, and a clown fish slaps its tail against my diving mask. Maybe it wants to scare away this great monster that is drifting a little too close to the sea anemones where he has his little home?

In silent worship I lift my hands towards the light far above. I have certainly been given treasures hidden in secret places in the ocean deep. The impossible has become possible. Freedom without barriers has guided my way to pearls of joy hidden in the deep darkness of the sea. I ascend towards the surface in motions like an invisible wind. A newborn joy has become mine. In a surge of bursting silver I emerge from the surface and laugh towards the golden light of the sun. It is as if I have opened the wrapping of the first day of the rest of my life.

A long time has now passed, however, since I went diving. In recent years hip problems and other limitations have put a temporary stop to my travels to the sea. Both San Andrés and the great blue deep have to wait. But the longing to dive again never disappears – the desire to once again shut the world outside and to drift through the calm, clear sea while glimmering air bubbles rise towards the surface far above. One day, some time, it will happen again. Waiting on a joy is also a joy.

26

Farewell

From time to time I am asked about the most difficult aspect of living in Colombia. One of the answers is that it is almost impossible to travel back to Europe at short notice. Since I need a wheelchair and need help with most of my daily activities, it is very hard for me to travel alone. It means that one of my personal assistants from Colombia needs to accompany me. For my own part the Norwegian passport opens most doors, but Colombians need a visa to travel to Europe. To obtain such a visa takes time, if it is ever granted. If my assistant receives a "No", I am also stopped. Through the years it has been painful when loved ones have wandered the last part of their life journey without my being able to be with them and say my last goodbye. Then instead I light a candle here in Colombia and keep a prayer vigil through long night hours. The person in question is not aware of it, but far away in South America there is someone who cares about them, and who is somehow present as their life is ebbing away.

I have often thought that prayer is like sending beams of light up into God's great mirror. Then He will perhaps turn the mirror slightly so the reflection of light is sent where darkness needs to be broken, to someone who needs God's care and presence at that moment.

I have become increasingly aware of how much the small details matter in ministry for God, and how important it is to obey what God says. I often wake up during late night hours without knowing why. Then I ask the Lord to show me who He would like me to pray for. Sometimes the answer is given as a face appears before me, and I can pray specifically for that individual. Later I might find out what happened there and then – how God intervened at the exact time. At other times I get no such answer.

While I write these words, it is again time for farewell here in Colombia. The suitcases are packed, and a long journey is at hand. This time serious illness in my immediate family has coincided with my planned holiday.

On the way to the airport the taxi driver is sticking his arm out of the window and waving hard and long to signal that he intends to turn left. A motorcyclist is rushing past while tooting with a sound that according to Griselda resembles a hoarse cockerel. There are many things that are done differently here in South America.

After arriving at the airport there are long police checks and painstaking investigation of luggage. Unfortunately, many people attempt to smuggle drugs from here, and in the fight against this evil the police are making an important effort.

Those who have showed up to say goodbye to Griselda and me create a ring. We join hands and pray for each other, for the Lord's protection and presence in everything that will happen – both for us who are leaving and those who stay.

On our way to the airplane in Armenia we see a rainbow appearing above the mountains, against the background of dark blue clouds. The captain announces that it will be a turbulent trip – and it will be. When we have a stopover in Bogota, we also see a rainbow, as a sign of God's faithfulness written in the clouds.[7] He is present with us who leave and with those who stay behind.

Strong wings soon lift us high above the lush landscape. It is stretched out beneath us like a patchwork of green shades. Yellow and blue spots reveal that it is time for the flowering of guayacáns.

---

7 See Genesis 9, 11-16

After a little while we pass towering mountains that suddenly turn into deep blue ocean. Carried in God's mighty arms, we are led to the other side of the Atlantic.

This morning when we left our home, swallows were dancing above a blue guayacán and the night rain gave the morning air a fresh, cool clarity. High in the air I spot the shadow of a great bird. El cóndor pasa – a condor flying past – and I wonder if it saw me as I could see it. What did it see in its bird's eye perspective? What was its view as it soared through the warm air currents on its mighty, still, outstretched wings? Did it see a greater scope?

Both the condor and I have a place in God's great creation. God is creating a puzzle, and my little piece of life has found its place in it – under a blue guayacán, where the wind's song laments, where the sun scatters the shadows after a long night, and where every day is a gift from my good heavenly Father!

27

Postlude

It is early in the morning. I am once again back on Gran Canaria. The brown, heavy wooden door opens. There stands Rafa! With mildly graying temples, he has become a little older than how I remember him. He has a mild expression on his face. Our eyes meet, and it is as if all the long years that have passed are erased. We stand completely silent, a long time. We just gaze at each other.

Then it is as if we come to life. Without words we embrace each other. It is like coming home after a long journey.

We walk along the beach. It is just before sunrise, and the city has hardly woken up. In the sand fishermen are about to pull ashore the multi-coloured boats with this night's catch. One of the boats has the name "Beatriz" written on the bow. A memory comes to mind. Once before I have seen fishermen pull ashore a boat with that name. An old, Catholic chorus streams into my thoughts:

Señor, me has mirado en los ojos,

sonriendo has dicho mi nombre.

En la arena he dejado a mi barca,

junto a ti buscaré otro mar.

Lord, you have looked into my eyes.

Smiling, you called me by name.

In the sand, I left my boat

to look for other seas together with you.

We slip into a pavement restaurant that has opened early. At a corner table, we are protected from the looks of busy people rushing past. Rafa and I each get a cup of hot chocolate, and while we enjoy fresh, warm *churros* we open doors that have been locked inside of us. In our corner of the café time is standing still, and a gentle, still joy is vibrating between us, as a rainbow of multi-coloured pieces of fabric *pareos* are fluttering on a stand outside on the promenade. This morning we both experience the faithfulness of God. Four hands are gripped together, and our gaze meets over the abyss of time and separation. There is pain, there is joy, here. So many days that have turned into long months and years are wiped out as we speak about what our lives have become. Storms have raged in our dark nights, but in spite of everything, God has let forgiveness flourish in our hearts. During these early hours the Lord breaks off chains of despair and bitterness. At the break of day He wraps us in His robe of peace. The dry wind rustles as it blows through the tall palm trees, and sun and shadows dance across golden skin. After the long winter of sorrow the fragile almond flowers of spring are finally budding.

It is a brief encounter in a moment of each of our lives. Time cannot be turned back. Many choices cannot be undone. Our life path is no longer as it was. But this day is ours, and only ours. Finally a shooting star draws a silent, shimmering line across the blue night sky. It is again time to say goodbye. God bends his ear to us, two of His small children, and our moment is fixed in eternity. Our Lord sees us. I think He is smiling towards us, He who knows that the best can only come out of great pain.

The sound of Rafa's steps slowly fade away at dusk, while the whisper of restrained tears is carried away by the night wind. Some choices are more difficult to make than others.

Strong hands carry me on board the plane that will take me the first part of the journey back to Colombia. After a short stay in Norway and Gran Canaria, the way again goes towards the south. The silvery wings of the aircraft lift into the sky as the sun sets over this day that soon will be just a memory. Blue sea is pounding against the black volcanic cliffs where foamy peaks are tossed into the air and coloured by the golden light of the sun that soon descends beneath the horizon. Silhouettes of dark mountains are erased in the night haze as the plane again begins the long journey across the Atlantic.

The large fuselage continues on underneath a night sky sprinkled with stars. A path through the dark hours of the night opens up to a new morning.

Jesus is still returning to Colombia – and on my four little wheels I am rolling together with Him.

Forgiveness

Forgiveness has 4 aspects:

1. Asking God for forgiveness: dealing with own sin
2. Forgiving oneself
3. Forgiving others
4. Making things right with God, if you have been unjust and blamed Him for painful and difficult things in life.

To ask God for forgiveness

Turning from the results of having been hurt / dealing with own sin that has been given room

Heavenly Father, I confess that as a result of having been hurt, I have allowed attitudes ... (e.g. hatred, bitterness, anger, rejection, condemnation, passivity, rebellion, self-condemnation etc.) to gain a foothold in my inner being and have control in my life. I acknowledge and confess my sin in this area, and I repent and turn away from it. I ask you, Jesus, to forgive me and cleanse me of such attitudes and thoughts. In Jesus' Name. Amen.

Forgiving oneself

Thank you, Father, that you forgive me because of Jesus Christ by grace alone.

Since *you* forgive me (for specific matters that have been confessed and dealt with), I now choose to forgive myself.

I choose not to accuse or punish myself in thought, speech or action, for the things you have now forgiven me for. In Jesus' Name. Amen.

Forgiving others

Thank you, Jesus, that you died for me so that I could be forgiven.

By the determination of my will I now choose to forgive those who have hurt me and caused me pain.

I choose to forgive .... (here you can mention them by name, softly on your lips)

for ... (be specific).

I release each and every one of them from my life and set them free in the Name of Jesus through my forgiveness. Amen.

In relation to God

Lord, forgive me for blaming you for the pain and hurt I have experienced in life, that does not come from you. It was not right of me to blame you. I know it is Satan who comes to steal, kill and destroy. You hate the plans and work of Satan. Forgive me, Lord, for accusing you for what others have done to me.

Thank you for sending Jesus to defeat evil. Thank you, Jesus, that you defeated evil when you died on the cross and rose from the grave. Thank you for loving me and setting me free. Amen.

Further Resources

Forgiveness, God's Master Key
– Pray the Most Powerful Prayer on Earth!

Peter Horrobin

Forgiveness is key to the restoration of our relationship with God and to healing from the consequences of hurtful, damaging human relationships. From the Cross, Jesus prayed these dramatic words to God, 'Father, forgive them, for they do not know what they are doing.' Learning to pray this powerful prayer is the beginning of a lifetime's adventure with God!
Paperback 112 pages, ISBN 9781852405021

A-Z Guide to the Healing Ministry

David Cross

With hundreds of definitions, inspirational commentaries and creative illustrations, David condenses the fundamental foundations of the healing and deliverance ministry of Jesus into highly readable sections, providing you with a mini-library of dynamic teaching. This invaluable reference book will empower and further your understanding of the healing and deliverance ministry and provide personal keys to help you in your own Christian walk.
Hardback 480 pages, ISBN 978-185240-755-1

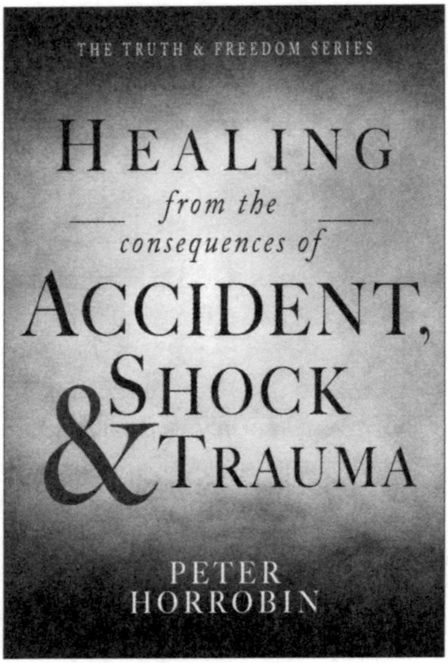

Healing from the consequences of Accident, Shock and Trauma

Peter Horrobin

Traumatic events leave a scar on broken lives. Unhealed trauma is one of the primary reasons why some people do not easily heal from the consequences of accidents or sudden shocks. This ground-breaking book is the culmination of thirty years of experience praying for such people. Peter carefully explains what trauma can do to people and how to pray for healing. This foundational teaching has been instrumental in bringing permanent healing to people all over the world. An essential manual for those who regularly pray for people – a life-transforming handbook for those who are struggling themselves with unresolved and unhealed issues – including the consequences of shock and injuries sustained in the military.
Paperback 176 pages, ISBN 9781852407438

Lynda

– From Accident & Trauma to Healing & Wholeness

Lynda Scott

Lynda's moving story of how God brought supernatural healing to every part of her spirit, soul and body will give you the capacity to transform your understanding of healing and give hope to those in need. Following a life-changing accident, Lynda retells the dramatic story that led to the powerful ministry that amazed witnessing doctors!
Paperback 152 pages, ISBN 9781852405397

Sarah

– From an Abusive Childhood and the Depths of Suicidal Despair to a Life of Hope and Freedom

Sarah Shaw

So many abused, hurting people are stuck in the tormenting symptoms of guilt and self-hatred, multiple fears, depression, Obsessive Compulsive Disorder, eating disorders, and even self-harming and suicidal tendencies. This book is a powerful story that has emerged from a background of extreme abuse and journals Sarah's road to healing.
Paperback 176 pages, ISBN 9781852405113

The Choice

– Serving Heaven or Serving Hell

Andy Robinson

Rejecting his Christian upbringing and wanting to satisfy his every pleasurable desire, the author turned away from a 'limiting' God and made a 'deal with the devil' who seemed to offer so much. Indulgence, pleasure and freedom seemed to satisfy until the day his world came crashing down. If your life feels out of control, this book offers that same hope that transformed Andy's life.
Paperback 144 pages, ISBN 9781852407117

In Rebel Hands

–The True Story of How God Spoke to a Group of Kidnapped Missionaries in the Jungles of Mozambique

Trish Perkins

The true, inspirational story of how God spoke to a group of six missionaries and a baby abducted at gunpoint in the jungles of Mozambique by heavily armed guerrilla soldiers. Trish Perkins underlines God's purposes at work in the deep heart of Africa's spiritual darkness and writes of the sense of hope even though held by violent captors.
Paperback 416 pages, ISBN 9781852405045

Keziah

– A Little Piece of God's Heart

Lizzie Grayson

A beautiful story of God's profound love for His children. Lizzie's book is written to give hope to anyone who has experienced the pain of losing a child and depicts the grief and loss endured by the author and her family. But the strength and faith they have in God ultimately pulls them through this tragic time.
Paperback, 144 pages ISBN 9781852405403

The Miracles of Pierrepont

Jill Southern-Jones with Kathleen McAnear-Smith

Jill Southern-Jones was the founding director of the work of Ellel Ministries at Ellel Pierrepont. In this wonderful book she shares of the miraculous details of her own faith journey alongside the story of the restoration of the property and the birthing of the NETS School. It's a momentous testimony to the power of trusting in God to meet ALL needs!
Paperback 192 pages, ISBN 9781852407407

There is Always Enough

Rolland and Heidi Baker

If you're searching for a demonstration of the Gospel then look no further than this miraculous story of one couple's journey and their team as they reach the poorest of the poor in Mozambique. This book gives a pure example of what can happen when love touches 'the least of these'.
Paperback 192 pages, ISBN 9781852405427

Unreachable
– A true story of one man's journey through drugs, violence, armed robbery and a miraculous encounter with God in prison

Darrell Tunningley

This compelling true story of the redemptive grace and mercy of God will surely pull you in right from the start! Darrell first met God in his prison cell and whilst in the prison he began to be used by the Lord instantly, helping others transform their broken lives through his example.
Paperback 96 pages, ISBN 9781852405892

The work of
Ellel Ministries International

Ellel Ministries was first established at Ellel Grange in the UK. The word Ellel is simply the name of the community in which Ellel Grange was built in the nineteenth century. In old English the word Ellel was *"All hail"* – meaning Praise God! In Hebrew it means *"towards God"* and in old Chinese the words mean *"Love flowing outwards"*.

For thirty years now God's love has been flowing outwards through the work bringing His healing to those in need and providing teaching and training for the Body of Christ. In the early days of the work people came from overseas and on returning home they began the work of establishing a local Ellel Center in their own country. Each one has the same vision to minister healing and to teach and train people to fulfil God's great commission in their local church.

Current list of centres, addresses and contact details:

UK Centers

Ellel Grange (& **International HQ**) Bay Horse, Lancaster, Lancashire, LA2 0HN
Tel: 01524 751 651 *Email:* info.grange@ellelministries.org

Ellel Glyndley Manor, Stone Cross, Pevensey, East Sussex, BN24 5BS
Tel: 01323 440 440 *Email:* info.glyndley@ellelministries.org

Ellel Pierrepont, Frensham, Farnham, Surrey, GU10 3DL
Tel: 01252 794 060 *Email:* info.pierrepont@ellelministries.org

Ellel Scotland, Blairmore House, Glass, Huntly, Aberdeenshire, AB54 4XH
Tel: 01466 799 102 *Email:* info.scotland@ellelministries.org

Ellel Ireland, 35 Beanstown Road, Lisburn, County Antrim, BT28 3JQS, Northern Ireland
Tel: +44 (0) 28 9260 7162 / 07545 696 750 *Email:* info.northernireland@ellelministries.org

Ellel Ministries Overseas Centers

Ellel Ministries Africa, PO Box 39569, Faerie Glen 0043, Pretoria, South Africa
Tel: +27 12 809 0031 / 1172 *Email:* info.africa@ellelministries.org

Ellel Kwazulu-Natal, PO Box 12, Winklespruit, 4145, KwaZulu-Natal, South Africa
Tel: +27 (0)31 916 2134 *Email:* bookingskzn@ellel.org.za

Ellel Ministries Australia (Sydney) Gilbulla, 710 Moreton Park Road, Menangle 2568, NSW, Australia
Tel: +61 02 4633 8102 *Email:* info.gilbulla@ellelministries.org

Ellel Ministries (Perth) PO Box 277, Gosnells, WA 6990, Australia
Tel: +61 (0)8 9398 4648 *Email:* info@wa.ellel.org.au

Ellel Ministries Canada in Ontario, 183 Hanna Road, RR#2, Westport, Ontario, K0G 1X0, Canada
Tel: +1 613 273 8700 *Email:* info.emc@ellelministries.org

Ellel Ministries Canada West, Prairie Winds Centre, RR1, Site 15, Comp. 42, Didsbury, Alberta, T0M 0W0 Canada
Tel: +1 403 335 4900 *Email:* info.calgary@ellelministries.org

Ellel Ministries France (La FraternitéChrétienne), 10 Avenue Jules Ferry, 38380 Saint Laurent du Pont, France
Tel: +33 47 65 54 266 *Email:* info.france@ellelministries.org

Ellel Ministries Germany e.V., Bahnhofstr. 45-47, 72213 Altensteig, Germany
Tel: +49 7453 275 51 *Email:* buero@ellelgerman.de

Ellel Ministries Hungary, Veresegyhaz, PF17, 2112, Hungary,
Tel/Fax: +36 28 362 396 *Email:* info.hungary@ellelministries.org

Ellel Ministries India, 502 Orchid Holy Cross Road, I. C. Colony, Borivili West, Mumbai, 400103, India
Mob: +91 93 2224 5209 *Email:* info.india@ellelministries.org

Ellel Ministries Malaysia - KL/Klang Valley, 9 & 11 Jalan Dendang 1, Kawasan 16, BerkeleyTown Center, 41300 Klang, Selangor D.E, Malaysia
Tel: +60 33 3599 011 *Email:* info.kl.malaysia@ellelministries.org

Ellel Ministries Malaysia - Sabah, Lot 10 and 12, First Floor, Wisma Leven, LorongMargosa 2, Luyang Phase 8, 88300 Kota Kinabalu, Sabah, Malaysia
Tel: +60 88 265 800 *Email:* info.malaysia@ellelministries.org

Ellel Ministries Netherlands, Wichmondseweg 19, 7223 LH Baak, The Netherlands
Tel: +31 575 441 452 *Email:* info.netherlands@ellelministries.org

Ellel Ministries New Zealand, PO Box 17690, Sumner, Christchurch 8840, New Zealand
Mob: +64 21 269 8384 *Email:* info.newzealand@ellelministries.org

Ellel Ministries Norway, Stiftelsen Ellel Ministries Norge, Groså̊s Senter, 4724 Iveland, Norge
Tel: +47 6741 3150 *Email:* post@ellelnorge.no

Ellel Papua New Guinea, C/o Boroko Baptist Church, PO Box 1689, Boroko, National Capital District 111, Papua New Guinea
Tel: +675 7161 3587/+675 767 33255 *Email:* info.png@ellelministries.org

Ellel Romania, Trotusului nr. 4, Oradea, 410242, Bihor, Romania
Tel: +40 731 351 445 *Email:* contact@ellelromania.ro

Ellel Ministries Rwanda, P.O. Box 2964, Kigali, Rwanda,
Tel: +250 789 501 986 *Email:* bookingsrwanda@ellel.org.za

Ellel Ministries Singapore, 39A JalanPemimpin, #05-01A, Halcyon Building, Singapore 577183
Tel: +65 6252 4234 *Email:* info@zion-ellel.org.sg

Ellel Ministries Sweden, Kvarnbackavägen 4 B, 711 92 Vedevåg, Sweden
Tel: +46 581 930 36 *Email:* info.sweden@ellelministries.org

Ellel Ministries Switzerland, Spitalweg 20, 4125 Riehen, Switzerland
Tel: +41 61 645 42 17 *Email:* info.switzerland@ellelministries.org

Ellel Ministries USA, 1708 English Acres Drive, Lithia, Florida 33547, USA
Tel: +1 813 737 4848 *Email:* info.usa@ellelministries.org

Would You Join With Us To Bless the Nations?

At the Sovereign World Trust, our mandate and passion is to send books, like the one you've just read, to *faithful leaders who can equip others* (2 Tim 2:2).

The 'Good News' is that in all of the poorest nations we reach, the Kingdom of God is growing in an accelerated way but, to further this Great Commission work, the Pastors and Leaders in these countries need good teaching resources in order to provide sound Biblical doctrine to their flock, their future generations and especially new converts.

If you could donate a copy of this or other titles from Sovereign World Ltd, you will be helping to supply much-needed resources to Pastors and Leaders in many countries.

Contact us for more information on (+44)(0)1732 851150 or visit our website www.sovereignworldtrust.org.uk

> *"I have all it takes to further my studies. Sovereign is making it all possible for me"*
>
> **Rev. Akfred Keyas – Kenya**

> *"My ministry is rising up gradually since I have been teaching people from these books"*
>
> **Pastor John Obaseki – Nigeria**

For more information about the worldwide work of Ellel Ministries please visit:

www.ellel.org